BASICS
FASHION DESIGN

Jenny Udale

TEXTILES AND FASHION

EXPLORING PRINTED TEXTILES, KNITWEAR, EMBROIDERY, MENSWEAR AND WOMENSWEAR

Second Edition

Fairchild Books

An imprint of Bloomsbury Publishing Plc

50 Bedford Square
London
WC1B 3DP
UK

1385 Broadway
New York
NY 10018
USA

www.bloomsbury.com

Bloomsbury is a registered trade mark of Bloomsbury Publishing Plc

First published 2014

British Library Cataloguing-in-Publication Data

A catalogue record for this book is available from the British Library.

ISBN
PB: 978-2-9404-9600-6
ePDF: 978-2-9404-4768-8

Library of Congress Cataloging-in-Publication Data

Udale, Jenny

Textiles and fashion : exploring printed textiles, knitwear, embroidery, menswear and womenswear
/ Jenny Udale. — Second edition. pages cm

"First published 2008"—Title page verso.

ISBN 978-2-940496-00-6 (paperback) — ISBN 978-2-940447-68-8 (ePDF)
1. Textile fabrics. 2. Textile design. 3. Fashion design. I. Title.

TS1765.U33 2014

677—dc23

2013031389

Design by ALL CAPS, UK

Printed and bound in China

0.1 Patrick Li
Texture and silhouette has been
created with layers of fabric in this
dress by Patrick Li.

Introduction 006–007

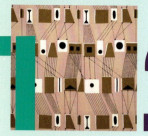

This book is for the textile designer who is interested in the integration of textile design with fashion and also the fashion designer who wants to fully integrate garment design with textiles. Designers who will consider how the scale of a design will work on the body, how the fabric will function on the body through drape or structure, and how the fabric will be cut and finished will benefit enormously from reading this book.

The book endeavours to cover all the things you need to know about fashion textiles. It begins with a brief history of textiles, showing the links with technical innovation and social developments. It then focuses on the processes of textile design, including the ethical and sustainable issues around textiles today. The book also provides practical information on fibre production, dyeing and finishing techniques. Also examined is how a fibre becomes a fabric through construction techniques, for example weave and knit, and other more innovative processes. The book continues by looking at the surface treatment of textiles including print, embroidery and embellishment, and then focuses on the way colour and trend can influence textiles and fashion. The final section gives practical information on the use of textiles within fashion design, and how to choose, cut and sew fabrics. Interviews with fashion and textile designers can be found within each chapter.

All the text in this book is underpinned with visual examples from designers who create wonderful textiles. I hope their work will inspire you and that you gain a great deal of pleasure from this book.

1 Comme des Garçons
A bold eclectic pattern is used on both shirt, shorts and jacket, large folds of fabric break up the graphic design.

It is important to consider what qualities are required for the textile you are designing before you start. Is it required for its aesthetic qualities and/or its function?

Aesthetically, you would need to think about how the textile drapes, the handle of the cloth, its texture, its colour, pattern or any surface interest. Also think about function: would the textile need to stretch around the body or be used for tailoring purposes? Is it needed for its protective qualities, perhaps against rain or the cold?

With the development of nano-textiles, more advanced functions can be catered for – a fabric might deposit a medicine on the skin or be a form of communication, as the colour changes according to the wearer's temperature or mood.

It is useful to have knowledge of the historical development and use of textiles, for example, how different fabrics and techniques have become fashionable within Western fashion. It is also interesting to see how textiles are used in different cultures to clothe the body. You should also be aware of the developments in future textiles: from ethical issues to smart materials.

The inspiration for textile design can come from any source and it can inform colour, texture, pattern and scale. Consider the ways in which you might begin designing, what media you might use – paint, pencil, CAD (computer-aided design) – and what surface you might work on. Once you have designed a range of textiles, it is important to consider how you might sell your ideas or manufacture the design as a length of fabric or a garment.

1.1 Dries Van Noten
Back stage at the catwalk show. This collection featured a variety of fabrications and pattern – transparent and opaque, printed and woven tartan, sequined and lace.

The Textile Sample

Looking back historically, we can see the types of textiles that were popular at certain times. This is usually related to an advancement in technology or trend within society. Throughout the history of textiles, certain patterns and fabrics have been repeated. These textiles become classics and some classics remain constantly popular in some form or another, for example, polka dots stripes and florals. Other classics go in and out of fashion, such as the paisley design. It is interesting to take a classic textile design and look at what makes it so timeless, and then try to reinvent it.

1.2

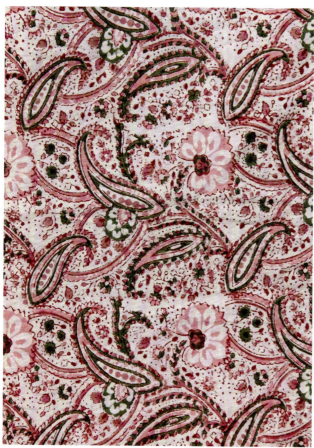

The Textile Sample

1.2 Paisley
A repeat design featuring the lozenge shapes we associate with a classic paisley.

1.3

1600s

The French Government supported the development of the silk industry in Lyon. New loom technology and dyeing techniques were developed that produced fine-quality silks, surpassing the Italian silks which had dominated the sixteenth century. The rococo period of the seventeenth century saw the fashion for very decorative dresses.

An offshoot of this was chinoiserie, where designs were inspired by the cultures and techniques of the East. Patterns were asymmetric, many featuring oriental motifs, and were exotic in their colour combinations. Japanese kimonos became very popular and were imported by the Dutch East India Company. This company also imported hand-printed cotton from India known as 'chintz'. It was a popular fabric as it was cheap, bright and colourfast. The popularity of the fabric threatened the French and British textile industries to such an extent that a ban on importing or wearing it was imposed.

Paisley

The paisley design developed from a stylized plant form seen on seventeenth- and eighteenth-century Indian cashmere shawls. During the nineteenth century, the town of Paisley in Scotland produced cashmere shawls featuring the design. The pattern has now become synonymous with the name paisley.

1.3 Indian chintz
Chintz wall hanging with a tree of life design.

1700s

In the early 1700s, 'bizarre silks' were popular. The exotic plant shapes found on them were the result of the influence of Eastern culture. They made way for lace motifs, then large-scale luxurious florals in the 1730s, moving to smaller sprays of flowers.

In 1759, the ban on chintz was lifted and the French textile industry again boomed. One factory in Jouy became famous for its printed cotton, the toile de Jouy. Louis XV's mistress, Madame de Pompadour, wore a type of silk known as *chiné à la branche* or pompadour taffeta. The silk had a water-blotting pattern effect, which was achieved by printing the warp before weaving the fabric.

During the eighteenth century, England dominated men's fashion due primarily to its superior wool manufacturing industry and skilled tailors, while France dominated women's fashion.

At the end of the eighteenth century, a simpler fashion to the rococo style became popular in women's clothing. A thin white cotton dress with little or no undergarments was worn, inspired by Greek and Roman antiquity. A muslin or gauze was best suited for this design as it offered a simple drape rather than moulding to the body. Cashmere shawls were worn over this garment in the winter. The shawls were brought back by Napoleon from his Egyptian campaign in 1799.

The cashmere shawl came from the region of Kashmir in north-west India. The wool of the mountain goat was spun into yarn to produce a light, soft, warm cloth of the highest quality. As a result, these shawls were very expensive. By the 1940s, the cashmere shawl had mass appeal and was made in small industries in France and Britain. Notably, Paisley in Scotland produced a less expensive shawl and the pattern became associated with the region.

1.4

1.4 Toile de Jouy design
Toile de Jouy designs originally depicted pastoral scenes that were finely rendered in one colour and positioned repeatedly on a pale background. In this example, Timorous Beasties have taken the landscape of modern-day London to produce a contemporary toile de Jouy design.

1.5a

1.5b

1.5a Cashmere shawl
White muslin walking dress with
high waist and a cashmere shawl.

**1.5b Madame de Pompadour
c. 1750**
A portrait of the Marquise de
Pompadour wearing a French-style
dress (Maurice-Quentin de la Tour,
Musée du Louvre, Paris, France).

1800s

Once again, the popularity of cotton in French fashion had grown to the point where it was threatening the silk industry and the French economy. So when Napoleon became Emperor in 1804 he instructed that silk and not cotton would be worn as the ceremonial dress. The Romantic period at the turn of the nineteenth century saw the use of small floral prints. They were popular for their aesthetics and also because the small designs easily hid dirt spots and poor manufacturing.

In 1834, Perrotine printing was invented and used for the mass production of cloth. This process was the mechanization of wood-block printing and allowed for multicoloured designs. Polychrome patterns that had previously been produced through woven cloth could now be produced through a cheaper printing method.

In the nineteenth century, lace manufacture was also mechanized. Large lace shawls made in the French towns of Valenciennes and Alençon became popular.

In the 1830s, the jacquard was widely used. This was produced on a mechanized drawn loom and allowed for more complex weave structures and patterns.

It was felt by some in the late nineteenth century that technical advancements and mechanization were responsible for a decline in the quality of design and crafts. Where a craftsperson had once been a designer and maker, the mechanized process was separating these two roles. The quality of textiles was poor and design was lacking. In Britain, William Morris was concerned with this situation and promoted handcrafted items over machine-manufactured ones. He designed textiles on naturalistic and medieval themes and chose not to use aniline dyes, preferring to dye them naturally. He was the most prominent member of the Arts and Crafts Movement in England.

Art nouveau developed from the Arts and Crafts Movement, with textiles becoming more stylized and intricately linear in design. Opening Japan to international trade in 1854 resulted in the Japanese style coming to the West. Oriental motifs and Eastern flora, like the ayame pattern (a flower from the iris family) and also the chrysanthemum, began to feature in textile design. Japanese lacquered products influenced the creation of shiny, lamé fabrics. In the 1860s, tarlatan, a thin plain, woven cotton, which was washed or printed with a starched glaze, was popular.

1900s

In the first quarter of the twentieth century, the Omega Workshops in London and Atelier Martine decorative art school and workshop in Paris opened. The Atelier Martine was founded by the couturier Paul Poiret, who was inspired by a visit to the Wiener Werkstätte school in Germany. The Atelier employed young girls with no design training, who produced very naive textiles. This approach and look was in-line with the fauvist and cubist movements of the time in the fine arts.

1.6

1.7

1.6 William Morris
Sunflower floral pattern entitled
'Evenlore Chintz'.

**1.7 Design by Atelier Martine
school for Paul Poiret c. 1919**
Block printed satin dress fabric.

1.8

1920s

After the discovery of Tutankhamun's tomb in 1922, Egyptian motifs were translated into textile designs. The art deco style originated from the Exposition Internationale des Arts Décoratifs et Industriels Modernes exhibition in Paris in 1925. Looser-shaped clothing became fashionable, influenced by the kimono shape and unstructured Eastern clothing. Madame Vionnet developed the bias cut, while Mariano Fortuny was inspired by classical clothing and created the pleated, unstructured Delphos dress.

During the roaring 1920s and the jazz era, the new dance crazes called for dresses made from fabrics that moved on the body or seemed to move under light. Fine, light fabrics, beading, sequins and fringing achieved this. Lace, fur and feathers were also popular for evening wear in this exciting and glamorous period. Viscose rayon was a popular fabric of the 1920s. This period also saw the introduction of the screen-printing process.

1.8 Dress c. 1925
An art deco style dress made from pink chiffon.

1930s

In the 1920s and 1930s, Coco Chanel used jersey in day dresses. This was revolutionary as this fabric had only been used before in underwear production. Florals, abstract and geometric patterns were popular, featuring two or more contrasting shades in a print. The development of cinema saw luxurious fabrics used for their lustre on-screen. Nylon was invented in 1935. Two-way stretch wovens were also developed during this decade. The cultural movement surrealism also influenced textiles.

The first sweater Elsa Schiaparelli displayed in her windows created a sensation: it was knitted in black with a trompe l'oeil white bow. She was a close friend of the artists Salvador Dalí, Jean Cocteau and Christian Bérard, and she commissioned them to design textiles and embroidery motifs for her dresses. Schiaparelli experimented with unusual fabrics in her designs, including the modern fabrics rayon, vinyl and cellophane.

1.9

1.9 Design by Elsa Schiaparelli
c. 1927
A hand-knitted wool jumper with a trompe l'oeil design of a bow cravat.

1940s

Fabric was rationed during the Second World War, so the amount used within a garment was conserved. For example, skirts were slim, not flared or pleated, and were a shorter length. Jackets were single breasted and trousers were a specific length. This was the era of 'make do and mend' with people recycling their textiles. Dresses were made from curtains, clothes were altered and knitwear was unravelled and re-knitted. Silk supplies from Japan were cut off during the war, so nylon became a popular substitute.

As France was occupied, Paris as a fashion capital was under threat and American fashions rose in popularity. Denim and gingham labourers' uniforms entered the ready-to-wear American market.

1950s

After the Second World War, there was a reaction against ornate pattern. Textiles featured futuristic imagery, scientific diagrams and bright, abstract shapes that echoed this atomic era. Textiles with linear drawings of newly designed domestic objects were also very fashionable. With the end of rationing, skirts became fuller and fuller. These circle skirts were often hand painted and embellished.

The influence of America on Europe also saw Hawaiian shirts and American prints becoming increasingly popular. Some of the couturiers, such as Balenciaga, created silhouettes that worked away from the body. They were interested in the space between the body and the garment. Stiffer fabrics worked well for this.

During the 1950s, new fabrics were also developed. These included acrylic (1950), polyester (1953) and spandex (1959).

1.10

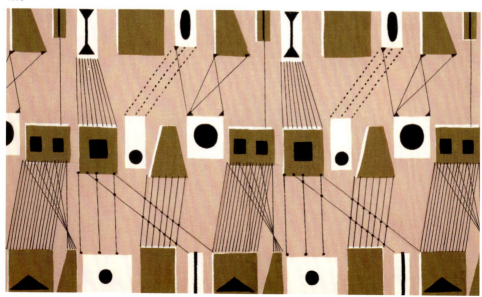

1.11

1960s

Baby boomers reached their teens and wanted to be different from their parents, so they chose to wear shorter skirts and modern fashions. Textiles were zany and came in bright colours. Space travel influenced bold prints and new synthetics with new dyes were being developed. Pierre Cardin and Paco Rabanne experimented with modern fabrications not seen in couture before. Trousers were normal daily dress for women. Jeans also became very popular, particularly amongst teenagers, as a result of American Western films and the influence of movie stars such as James Dean. Towards the end of the 1960s, there was a nostalgic look back to the art deco and art nouveau periods. Imagery was enlarged and translated into bright psychedelic colours. Florals were depicted flatter and with bold colour, and the term 'flower power' was coined. The work of Finnish designer Marimekko illustrates this very well.

1.10 Design by Lucienne Day
c. 1953
Screen printed linen for Heals Ltd featuring an abstract graphic design.

1.11 Design by Balenciaga c. 1963
This evening cape, made from white gazar fabric, has been designed with a strong simple silhouette that sits away from the body.

1970s

The unisex hippie folk movement of the 1970s was a reaction to the modernism and mass consumption of the 1960s and was triggered by the Vietnam War. The anti-establishment looked to different non-Western cultures and religions for inspiration and enlightenment. Fashionable men wore bright colours, lace and frills. The oil crisis of the 1970s contributed to the downturn of the synthetic fibre market in Britain. Natural fabrics were increasingly adopted. In the UK, Laura Ashley produced hand-printed looking cotton with Victorian florals.

1980s

During the 1980s, the UK was politically and economically more stable and fashion followed suit, adopting a more conservative approach. In 1979, Margaret Thatcher became the first female prime minister of Great Britain. More women were working and they chose to wear tailored suits with large shoulders. The term 'power dressing' was coined.

There was also a body-conscious trend with underwear worn as outerwear. Gaultier famously designed Madonna's conical bra outfits for her world tour in 1990. Azzedine Alaïa and Bodymap designed using the stretch fabric Lycra to contour the body.

Japanese designers Rei Kawakubo and Yohji Yamamoto developed a new trend. Garments were not body conscious, but played with interesting cut. Fabrics were monochrome, non-decorative and, in some cases, torn and raw. Recycled cotton was also introduced.

1.12

1.12 1970s' textile design
Hand embroidered with thick natural yarns to give a textured folkish look.

1.13 Design by Rei Kawakubo (Comme des Garçons) 1982
Controlled holes have been hand knitted into this sweater to give a deconstructed aged look.

The Textile Sample

1.13

1990s

The trend started by the Japanese designers continued and was also taken up by a handful of Belgian designers. Martin Margiela was one of them; he worked in a conceptual way and wanted his clothes to look handmade, not mass-produced. He used deconstruction and recycling throughout his collections. Ripped denim and customization became mainstream.

2000s

Textiles have become more and more decorative as production is taken to the Far East and China. The factories here can add value to a textile through embellishment; the workers are skilled (often using local crafts) and the fabric can be produced cheaply.

Modern fabrics are developing so that they are light-sensitive and breathable. Computer-aided design and manufacture are common. The designer is now far more in control of the mechanization process; however, as a result, craft skills are unfortunately declining in Europe.

Developments in the creation of textiles seem to be following two paths: ethically driven by the environment and future technologies driven by scientific advances – and where they meet is where great future fabrics will be produced. In other words, sustainable fabrics that use great design, but can also be forward thinking.

We should also consider how traditional crafts, such as block printing, hand crochet and crewel work, can be maintained. These handicrafts give textiles character and individuality, and they can add value to a product as a result of the time and skill needed to create it. A garment that has been hand stitched and embroidered will never be exactly the same as another garment. Certainly, high-end designers are incorporating hand-crafted fabrics and finishes into their collections, but these handicraft techniques are difficult for the high street to copy and therefore set them apart. Consumers, however, are demanding fabrics that can perform well and that can wash and wear well, so maybe combining craft with performance and modern technologies will ensure their survival.

1.14

1.14 Design by Xiao Li
This outfit incorporates new ways to produce textiles from silicone.

Ethics

Clothing is becoming cheaper as production is getting larger. We are buying our clothing in supermarkets with our weekly food shop. We are wearing a T-shirt a few times and throwing it away to buy the next desirable cheap garment. Fashion has a short shelf life with main season collections every six months, but also smaller selling collections available in between to keep the consumer interested. If the season's collections do not sell in the season they go on sale, they are burnt or recycled.

One reaction to this mass consumption is the rise of sustainable collections. Companies are considering the impact that their textiles and processes have on the environment. Many are choosing to use fabrics that are made from recycled materials, either at fibre or fabric level. Many fibres come from natural sources and can be reused; some synthetic fibres can also be recycled, for example polyester can be made from old plastic bottles.

Dye companies that use synthetic dyes are reducing the amount of chemicals that are needed in processes and recycling the water they use, so reducing the impact of production. Synthetic dyeing is often seen as unethical. However, natural dyes need fixers that can be harmful to the environment as they build up; also, some natural dyes need a large amount of natural material to produce a small amount of dye.

There has been a trend for organic and fairtrade in industries such as food and cosmetics, but the fashion industry has been slower to pick up on the idea.

Some may say that fashion is fundamentally about aesthetics, so is there room in fashion for ethics? It is important that ethical companies integrate functionality, design and quality into their ethical story for their products to be fashionable and desirable. They will, however, be competing with low-price manufacturers who are churning out products more cheaply and quickly than before.

As a designer, you can choose where you buy your textiles or where you have your textiles manufactured. It may be harder to source sustainable or ethical materials, and it may make your designs more expensive. You may be competing with cheaper goods from non-certified factories, but ultimately it is your choice. Decide how much you want to be involved with the issues, but educate yourself.

Fairtrade

The term 'fairtrade' is part of the Fairtrade
Foundation's logo and is used to refer to
products that have actually been certified
'fairtrade'. The Fairtrade Foundation gives
this certification after it checks that the
growers or workers have been given fair pay
and treatment for their contribution to the
making of the product.

The working environment in which the
products are made is taken into account.
Manufacturers have to demonstrate that they
provide good conditions for the people
involved in the factory. There are basic
standards covering workers' pay and
conditions, as well as issues such as the
absolute prohibition of the use of child labour,
which must be met in order to qualify for the
fairtrade 'kite mark'.

Fairtrade is also used to describe products
that try to encourage the use of natural and
sustainable materials, together with
contemporary design to maintain ancient
skills and traditional crafts, where regular
employment and the development of
skills can bring dignity back to people
and their communities.

1.15

1.15 Knitwear by Nikki Gabriel
Gabriel has developed a yarn she
calls 'Wooli', made from factory fibre
waste that is carded, respun and
recycled.

1.16

Organic

The General Assembly of the International Federation of Organic Agriculture Movements (IFOAM) is the worldwide organization of the organic movement, uniting 870 member organizations in 120 countries. IFOAM's goals are the worldwide adoption of ecologically, socially and economically sound systems that are based on the principles of organic agriculture. The principles aim to protect the land that is being farmed and also those working on it and the communities of which they are a part. Strict regulations define what organic farmers can and cannot do, placing strong emphasis on protecting the environment. They use crop rotation to make the soil more fertile, they cannot grow genetically modified crops and only use – as a last resort – natural pesticides to control pests and diseases. (See Chapter 2: Fibres, for more information on organic cotton production.)

Animal rights

The campaign for animal rights gets stronger every year, yet designers continue to show catwalk collections that contain fur. There still seems to be a demand from a certain consumer group for fur in fashion. Designers are now using fur and leather substitutes in experimental ways. Stella McCartney does not use any animal products in her collections; instead, she uses canvas and fake leather in her accessories. There is a lot of research into developing good leather-look fabrics. The Japanese company Kuraray produces Clarino and Sofrina, and the company Kolon Fibers produces an ultra-microfibre textile called Rojel.

1.16 Design by Kuyuchi
The brand aim to make their collection as sustainable as possible. They are constantly experimenting with new sustainable concepts like recycled polyester, Tencel®, spare denim and hemp.

Technology

Technology is being used to generate new fabrics and also to produce existing fabrics more quickly and efficiently. The possibilities of futuristic textiles are positively endless.

Smart materials

Interactive clothing incorporates smart materials that respond to changes in the environment or to the human body. Heat, light, pressure, magnetic forces, electricity or heart rate may cause changes to the shape, colour, sound or size of materials. It is especially appropriate to textiles, as during the construction process, fibres and yarns can form circuits and communication networks through which information is transferred.

Coating finishes, printing and embroidery can also all be used to conduct information. Clothes could quite possibly interact directly with the environment by opening doors or switching on lights, or could communicate with images, light or noise.

Biotechnology

Fabrics can contain chemicals within their fibres that can be released onto the skin for medicinal or cosmetic reasons. Fibres are being developed from natural sources to mimic nature, for example the development of spider silk; this natural fibre is three to five times stronger than steel and is stretchy and waterproof. Biochemists are researching its structure and developing synthesized fibres. Fabrics are also being grown directly from fibres in the same way that skin or bones grow.

CAD

Digital technology and computer-aided design (CAD) is advancing and making the designer's job easier. Designing a textile sample using CAD can produce a repeat in many colours far quicker than if done by hand. Computerized looms can produce metres of fabric in minutes. Obviously, manufacturing processes must evolve, but it is important to still understand the craft techniques on which these processes are based.

1.17a

1.17b

1.17a Biocouture
An experiment in growing shoes
and other fashion garments using
living organisms like bacteria and
yeast to grow materials directly into
finished products.

**1.17b Brooke Roberts
'Calibration' collection**
Inspired by X-ray imaging, the top
and trousers were knitted using a
digital stoll knitting machine with a
Jaquard programme.

Engaging research is the first stage to designing innovative textiles. It is important to find a way to document and express your findings and ideas through drawing, collage, photography or maybe CAD work. From your research, will you start to design your samples on paper initially and then develop into cloth and knit? Or will you start to work directly with materials?

As you design, you must understand the basic textile design principles of scale, texture, colour, pattern, repeat, placement and weight. Consider how these principles work within a sample and how these samples work together as ranges. Consider also how your designs will result in functional, inspirational or commercial textiles suitable for use within contemporary fashion design and garment construction.

Researching textiles

In order to design original textiles you must first undergo a process of research. Research is an indulgent, but important time that enables you to delve into topics and areas of interest to stimulate you creatively.

Your primary research can come from anything – historical costume and textiles, craft, nature or architecture, and you could start with looking on the Internet and books (from the library or your own collection), but often the most exciting research is done by experiencing places, countries, museums and flea markets, places where you can take photos, draw or gather objects.

Your research might take the form of a theme, such as art deco, which is quite visual in its research as you might look at an art deco building or go to an exhibition. You could, however, have a more conceptual approach to your research. For example, by using the idea of 'motion' you could look at how wind moves objects and creates volume and shapes, or perhaps see how a pen attached to piece of string could create patterns when swung and left to the forces of gravity and motion.

Research that has a narrative or story behind or through it could also generate more personal abstract ideas.

Whichever approach you take, it is important that your research really engages you and gives you enough interesting information for your designing. It should be able to stimulate ideas for imagery, pattern, texture, colour and (for garment design) silhouette and detail.

As well as the primary or original research we have just discussed, it is important that you also look at what is happening in fashion and textiles currently; this is known as secondary research. This will enable you to direct your designs: Do you want to do something similar to what is happening currently, to follow a trend and to be fashionable? Or do you want to react against current ideas?

The Textile Sample

1.18 Moodboard
Moodboard by Annie Ovrachenko
showing research into ethnic
garments, featuring neck
and sleeve details.

1.18

Sketchbooks and mood/ research boards

The next step is to collate the research that you have gathered. Documenting your exciting findings tends to be done firstly in a sketchbook where images, photographs, fabrics, yarns and drawings are placed together to form connections on a page and a journey of ideas through the book that will develop into design ideas. Collage, dissect, write and draw, and respond to the images and things you have gathered. You should be developing and communicating your ideas here (not too much writing though, as designers we would rather see images than read loads of text). Your sample textile ideas on fabric or in knit could also go in your sketchbook.

Your sketchbook will be very useful in creating mood or research boards. You will need to carefully select your most important images and information that best reflect your research. A mood or research board should clearly sum up and effectively communicate your message to whoever is looking at it. The next step is to develop more focused design ideas.

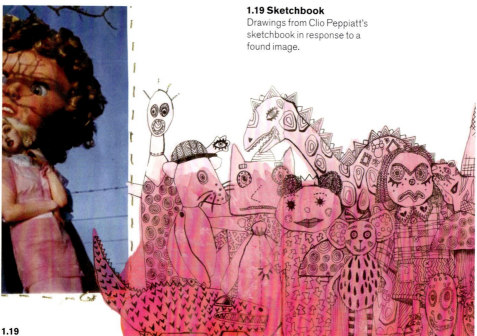

1.19 Sketchbook
Drawings from Clio Peppiatt's sketchbook in response to a found image.

1.20

Rendering designs

You now need to think about what you are trying to design and how best to go about it. Determining the most appropriate medium in which to render your designs in is very important, whether it is paper, paint, pencils or a software package. Work out what is required and in what time frame. Bear in mind that you might need to learn new skills for the designs you are creating. Always remember to experiment and enjoy the process.

Drawing

Being able to communicate your ideas through drawing is fundamental to most design disciplines. However, it is also possible to use other media, such as collage and photography, as a means of communication. Experiment with drawing; use different types of media, and be expressive with line, colour and texture. Think also about silhouettes and blocks of colour or tone within your design. Consider whether you are trying to represent what you are drawing precisely or if the artwork is developing in a more abstract direction.

1.20–1.21 Artwork ideas
Different types of drawing and mark making which Emma Wright combines together to make a final design.

1.21

Collage and 3D rendering

Working with different types of papers and building up layers to create textures can be useful for knit and weave ideas. Try finding unusual textures to play with, but remember to refer back to the function of your fabric. You might try to experiment and mock up a sample in a fabrication similar to the yarn you might eventually use.

Computer-aided design (CAD)

The use of the computer can make the design process faster. Colour and scale can be changed more quickly than manually recolouring or rescaling a design. Remember that colours on a computer screen are different from those eventually printed out, as the computer screen works with light and not pigment. Scanning original drawings and combining them with other imagery can work well. Avoid using filters and treatments from design packages unless they are used originally, otherwise they can look very obvious. Packages that can quickly put designs into repeat are great, but again must be used carefully or the repeat can look very uninspiring.

1.22

Photography

Using photography is a good way to capture ideas quickly. Textures and shapes can be registered in great detail immediately without the need for hours of drawing. By using packages such as Photoshop, images can now be successfully translated into designs. Layers and collages can be built up on screen.

1.22 Digital artwork idea
Feathers have been scanned in and manipulated to create a pattern.

1.23 A-lab Milano
Outfit featuring a digitally manipulated and printed textile design.

It is important that as a designer you understand the basic principles of textile design. This knowledge will allow you to explore fully the design process. Obviously, some samples will feature certain principles more than others. Think about how you might apply the following principles in this chapter to your designs. For example, you might produce a range of black samples that focuses on the application of shiny surfaces to matt-base cloths. The juxtaposition of surfaces and placement of pattern might be the focal point of these designs rather than colour.

Scale

Look at the scale of your design within the fabric piece. Is it very small and repeated or is it enlarged and abstract? You may consider placing a large design with a smaller design for added contrast. Think about how this design will work on the body and how it will work within the pattern pieces of a garment. An enlarged bold design may not have as much impact if the design has to be cut up to be used in a garment with many pattern pieces. Think how you can place a large design within a garment silhouette for the best effect.

1.24 Print scale
Sketches showing scale and placement ideas for print by Emma de Vries.

1.24

DIGI PRINT SAMPLE
Silk Shantung/Cream

The Textile Sample

1.25

Pattern and repeat

If you would like your textile sample to work down a length of fabric you must consider how it repeats. Repeats can be very simple or very complicated working across a large area. The bigger the repeat, the harder it is to see on a length of fabric; a small repeat is more obvious. It is important to observe how your design flows across a length. When you repeat your design en masse, you might find that you can see where you are clearly repeating the motif. This might work in a design or it might look rather crude. Also consider if there is a direction to your design. Is there a top and a bottom? This can look very interesting visually, but remember that this kind of design limits the lie of a fabric, as the pattern pieces will all have to be placed in one direction.

If you are working on a computer, it is very easy to see how your design will work by cutting and pasting. There are also computer packages that quickly put your design into repeat, look at the rhythm of the repeat across the screen and how this will translate onto a length of fabric. To work out manually whether your designs flow, cut the design in half and place the top part below the bottom to see where you need to fill in gaps.

1.25–1.26 Types of pattern
These Liberty print designs by Duncan Cheetham show an all-over floral pattern (1.25) and a chevron print (1.26). The chevron design has a 'direction', a clear top and bottom to the design.

1.26

Placements and engineered designs

Placements work well if you consider the position of the design on the garment. The most obvious placement is a print placed on the front of a T-shirt. It is interesting to consider how a design can be engineered to work around a garment. Can a seam be moved to allow a design to travel from the front to the back of a garment? Could a placement work around the neck or around an armhole? Can a design fit into a specific pattern piece? If you are working in this way, you may have to consider how the engineered design scales up or down according to the size of the garment. A size 10 garment will have a smaller neck hole than a size 14. You will have to produce a different size design for each dress size for this to really work. If you are working on the computer, this is much easier as designs can be scaled quickly and placed within pattern pieces.

Clever use of placements might affect the construction of the final garment. For example, a coloured block could be knitted directly into a garment, which would mean a coloured panel would not need to be cut and sewn in. A weave could incorporate an area of elastic running across it, thereby avoiding darting in the final garment to fit it to the body. Smocking applied to a fabric can work in a similar way.

1.27

1.27 Givenchy
This design from a Givenchy collection contains a striking use of placement. The circles on the jacket are placed so they correspond to the circles found on the blouse and shorts beneath. The circles on the front of the jacket also align with those on the sleeves and cuffs.

1.28　　　　　　　　　1.30

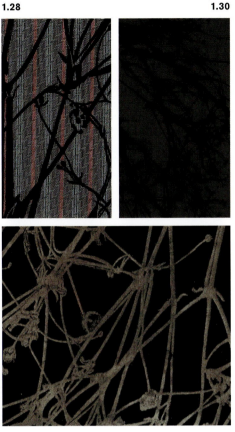

1.29

Colour and colourways

When you design, consider the various tones and saturations that can be found within one colour. Also experiment with the different textures of a hue. For example, the colour black can be blue-black, warm black, washed-out black, matt black, shiny black, or transparent black. Your palette will change under different lighting conditions – natural light at certain times of the day and different forms of electric lighting will all have an effect.

Weight, texture and surface

When you start to transfer your designs onto or into fabric, think about what weight your textile will be in relation to the design and also in relation to its use in the final garment. Understanding fabrics and yarns is paramount to this process (this will be explored more, later in this book).

Consider whether your design would benefit from texture. Surface interest is very important within textile design, especially in knit, embroidery and embellishment. In knit and weave design, the weight of the yarn and the size and type of stitch or weave will affect the texture. For printed textiles, surface interest is achieved through printing. Some printing media will sit on top of the fabric and produce a relief effect, while others might eat away at the surface of the textile through a chemical reaction.

The type of embellishment and the yarn or stitch used will produce various textures on embroidered fabrics. Mechanical and chemical finishing processes can change the texture of a fabric after it has been created. Interesting textiles can be created by experimenting with a mixture of processes, for example, pleating a fabric before you print onto it, or knitting a fabric then boiling it to give a matted texture.

1.28–1.30 Tonal prints
These prints by Jenny Udale show a matt print on a shiny fabric. Puff adds surface interest and the colours work well together.

As a student, you will be creating small textile samples and developing experimental and exciting ideas. You will probably only have to produce a small length of fabric or a small range of garments that feature your fabrics. However, when you become a designer in the fashion industry you will have to consider how to sell your work. If you choose to manufacture your textiles, you will also have to consider the skills and technology you will need for production, and the ethical choices you might make. You must consider how your textiles now work together and form a collection; then to whom you will present the samples and where you will sell them.

Collection of fabrics

When you create a collection of fabrics you must consider how the designs work together and what their common theme is. Are you creating a collection of similar designs, for example a range of striped textiles or a variety of designs – a stripe, spot and floral – that are maybe all rendered by a similar drawing technique? Consider how your range of designs works within a fashion collection: do you have all the different weights and qualities needed for all the garments? The colour palette is usually common to a range of fabrics, but you can vary the proportion of colour used in each sample within the range.

Try hard not to repeat a motif in a collection of designs. For example, you might think each design is very different, that in one design your motif of, say, a leaf, is small and lime green and in the next design it is large and black, but one company may buy the first design and another the second, and their designers could then resize and recolour your designs and end up with similar textile designs.

1.31 Fabric collection
A selection of fabrics used within a spring summer collection showing a variety of weights, textures and patterns. They all work together in a selected colour palette.

1.32 Line-up
This collection is presented with fabric swatches beneath each look, for easy identification of garment fabrication.

The Textile Sample

1.31

Presentation

Textile samples tend to be presented on hangers or simply mounted on light card fixed at the back. It is important that the textile is not stuck down, as it needs to be handled. Therefore, usually only one edge is attached to the mount leaving the fabric sample hanging, so the weight and drape can be experienced. Keep the mounting plain and simple so it does not distract attention away from the textile design. It is not normally advisable to present your samples in portfolio plastic sleeves as the fabrics cannot be easily handled.

1.32

Fabric fairs

Fabric trade fairs are held biannually in line with the fashion calendar. The fairs showcase new developments in woven, knitted, printed and embellished fabrics.

Première Vision (PV) is the main fabric and colour fair held biannually in Paris, France. Fabric manufacturers from around the world display their new fabric samples and take orders from designers. Sample lengths of fabrics are made first by the manufacturer and sent out to the designer. From these lengths, garment samples are made and orders from stores are taken by the designer. Fabric is then ordered for production of the garments. However, the fabric manufacture needs to reach a certain quantity of fabric orders to then put the fabric into production.

Indigo, also held in Paris at the same time as PV, is a platform for textile designers (mainly print designers) to show their textile samples. The samples are shown as collections and are bought by designers for inspiration, or by fabric companies and fashion companies to be put into production.

Pitti Filati is a biannual yarn fair held in Florence, Italy. Here, yarn companies display their latest collections of yarns for production and textile designers sell their knitted and woven samples. The other main yarn fair is Expofil in Paris.

If you choose to represent yourself at a fabric fair you must consider the cost of travel, hiring a stand at the exhibition, manning the stand and accommodation while you are there. If an agent takes your work to sell, they will take a percentage of the sales of your samples to cover their expenses; ask how long it will take to receive your payment. Always keep a good record of the samples that you give to an agent: take a photo, number each sample on the back and list the ones that are going. Get the agent to confirm and sign the list.

1.33a

1.33b

1.33c

The Textile Sample

1.33a–1.33c
Prints by Duncan Cheetham
Various designs showing repeat and placement.

Duncan Cheetham

What is your job title?
I am the senior print designer.

Please describe your job.
I work across menswear and womenswear runway and ready-to-wear prints. I also work on soft accessories.

What was your career path to your current job?
I received a BA (Hons) from UCE Birmingham, UK and an MA in printed textiles at the Royal College of Art, UK. I then worked in print design as a freelancer before becoming print designer at Liberty for eight years.

What do you do on an average day?
I work on a number of different divisions and it depends on the calendar whether I am working on men's, women's or scarves, or all three! I can be researching for design ideas, drawing development, colouring textiles I have designed in the seasonal palettes, or launching textile designs or scarf designs with the suppliers.

What are the essential qualities needed for your job?
You have to be extremely organized. Having relevant CAD skills is essential. You have to be versatile – colour and research should be intuitive and speedy!

How creative a job do you have?
My job is very creative even in a very large commercial company. It involves drawing and painting, initial research, and fabric development and experimentation.

How far in advance are you working on prints?
We work up to nine or ten months in advance on the printed textiles.

Do technological advancements in printing machines affect the kind of samples you design?
New printing technology does affect the design process, for example reversible digital printing is now possible. Digital printing has the least limitations for repeat size and number of colours, and is great for experimenting. I think the quality is improving all the time.

How have print trends changed over the last few years?
There is more digital photographic work. Trends come from innovative fashion designers and they filter through quickly online.

How do you put a collection of prints together?
I start with editorial and concept research and mix initial drawing, studies and paintings on large print boards. From these boards, final designs are selected for development, put into repeat, placement or scarf layout, and then coloured into the relevant palettes.

What determines the colour palette you use?
Our colour palettes are developed in-house.

Do you follow trends or do you go with your instinct?
Luxe fashion companies don't tend to follow trends. Brand identity evolves naturally. The creative director works with a number of themes and brand heritage.

What advice would you give someone wanting a job in your area of fashion?
You should gain as much experience as possible; this will help you decide the area of printed textiles you want to work in. Drawing practice is of utmost importance as a print designer.

1.34–1.35 Textile ideas
Here research is inspiring
fabric experimentations.
A new fabric has been constructed
by layering cut yarn and a
transparent fabric onto a wool base.
Random wool stitchwork has been
applied to this pulled silk chiffon.

**In this chapter, you have looked at examples of
historical textile samples and also how to start
designing your own textiles. The following projects
explore the process of designing a textile through
research of a historical or original nature, rendition
of ideas through drawing techniques, to mocking up
sample ideas.**

Project A: Research

Step 1: Visit a thrift store, garage sale or
your loft. Look for approximately five unusual
objects that interest you for their colour,
texture or shape. They could be five objects
of the same type or five very different and
contrasting items.

Step 2: Group your objects together. Gather
a range of drawing materials, pencils,
coloured pencils, paints, brushes, coloured
paper, and textured papers and cards.

Step 3: Start to draw. Work in a speedy way,
and do not spend hours carefully drawing the
objects realistically. Instead, respond to them
in a more experimental way.

For example, work with papers to create a
collage of tone or colour. Maybe draw the
objects, but with a single line, not taking your
pencil/pen off the page.

Take your objects and use them to create
artwork, so you could print with them or draw
around them.

Create textures. For example, if you had five
pairs of trainers, rather than drawing each
one precisely, it might be interesting to put
the soles of the shoes in ink and print the
texture of the tread. If you were a knit
student, this way of working would be more
useful to get ideas for creating a knit sample
than a line drawing of the shoe.

Create around ten artworks; do not work in a
sketchbook as this could restrict the size of
your artworks. Also, you will have to wait for
the artworks to dry before moving onto the
next page.

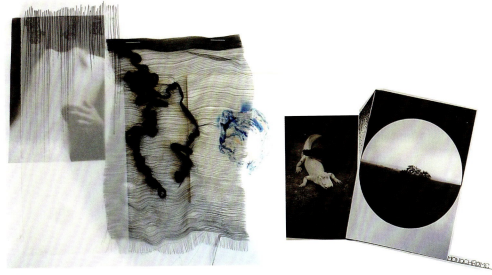

1.35

Project B: Translating your ideas

Step 1: Put your artworks up on a wall or spread them out on a table, so that you can see everything you have done. Now think about how these ideas could be translated into textile samples. Take a sketchbook and list fabrics that you need to source or yarns you could work with. These fabrics could be found at home or in a thrift store, or could be bought new.

Step 2: Once you have gathered your fabrics or yarns, start to respond to your artwork and create new samples. For example, from a textural artwork you could pleat, boil, tuft or stitch a fabric, or knit or crochet with yarn.

From a tonal colour-blocked collage, you could abstract a specific part and then create a textile from appliquéd fabrics. You could also layer fabrics and cut away layers, uncovering what is below.

From a line drawing you could draw directly onto a fabric with a ballpoint pen or draw with stitch lines.

Be experimental. Do not think your new textile samples have to be 100 per cent wearable, but do try and keep a good tactile quality to them. Have fun!

You should create around eight samples that are of good quality.

Step 3: Take five of the samples and group them together as a story, so they could be used within a collection; they could be five similar samples or they could be five contrasting ones.

Step 4: The next time you design a fashion collection, use the samples within your designs. They should inform your garment ideas. For example, if all your fabrics are quite heavy, then use them for outerwear or bags.

Fabrics are made, fundamentally, from fibres. These fibres can be categorized simply as natural or synthetic and each fibre has its own characteristics and qualities. For example, cotton fibres produce a fabric that is breathable, while wool fibres create a warm cloth, but one that can be sensitive to heat.

The way the fibres are spun and the yarn is constructed affect the performance and look of the final fabric. Finishes and treatments can be applied to a textile at the fibre, yarn, cloth or final garment stage of production. These finishes can enhance and change the qualities of the textile for fashion. Colour, texture and performance qualities can all be added. Obviously, the way the fabric is constructed also gives the fabric a specific quality. This will be discussed in the next chapter.

Companies who manufacture man-made and natural fabrics are considering their impact on the environment with their manufacturing processes. It is not as simple as natural fabrics are good for the environment and man-made are bad, as the production of natural fabric may use harmful chemicals in its processes; also, many man-made fabrics can now be completely recycled. Fabric characteristics can be integrated into the make-up of man-made fibres reducing the need for chemical and mechanical finishing processes.

2.1 Philip Lim
Embossed neoprene coat with leather skirt and angora sweater, colour blocked in pink, camel, oatmeal and black.

Fibres

Natural fibres are derived from organic sources. These can be divided into plant sources (composed of cellulose), or animal sources, which are composed of protein.

2.2

Cellulose

Cellulose is made of carbohydrate and forms the main part of plant cell walls. It can be extracted from a variety of plant forms to make fibres suitable for textile production. Here, we are looking at fabrics that are most suitable for the production of garments; they must be soft enough to wear and not break up when worn or washed.

2.2 Fabric swatches
Top row (from left to right): silk organza, silk jersey, raw silk, dupion silk; wool herringbone, melton wool; shearling, leather, horse hair.
Bottom row (from left to right):
foil-printed linen, linen;
denim, cotton shirting; bamboo, jute hessian.

Cotton

Cotton is a prime example of a plant fibre. It has soft, 'fluffy' characteristics and grows around the seed of the cotton plant. These fibres are harvested from the plant, processed and then spun into cotton yarn.

Cotton's enduring popularity is its extreme versatility; it can be woven or knitted into a variety of weights. It is durable and has breathable properties, which is useful in hot climates as it absorbs moisture and dries off easily. The longer the fibre, the stronger and better quality the fabric is, for example Egyptian cotton.

Cotton is mainly produced in the USA, China, the former Soviet Union, India, Mexico, Brazil, Peru, Egypt and Turkey. In most cotton production, farmers use chemical fertilizers and pesticides on the soil and spray them on the plants in order to prevent disease, improve the soil and increase their harvest. Cotton has always been extremely prone to insect attack and since insects started building up immunity to pesticides, the situation has worsened. This means growers have increased their use of chemical pesticides simply to ensure crop survival. Cotton crops in India, America and China demand thousands of tonnes of pesticides, which are sprayed on fields from the air. This overuse of pesticides is rendering hundreds of acres of land infertile and contaminating drinking water. The World Health Organization estimates that about 220,000 people die each year as a result of pesticide use.

Also, the chemicals that are used are absorbed by the cotton plant and remain in the cotton during manufacture, which means that it is still in the fabric that we wear next to our skin. Due to these issues, manufacturers are increasingly developing organic fibres that are grown and processed without the use of artificial fertilizers and pesticides. Organic fabric production is more expensive, but it has a low impact on the environment and is healthier for the consumer. There are designers pursuing organic solutions such as Katharine Hamnett, Wildlifeworks and Edun.

Linen

Linen has similar properties to cotton, especially in the way it handles, although it tends to crease more easily. Linen has good absorbency and washes well. It is produced from the flax plant and is commonly regarded as the most ancient fibre.

Hemp, ramie and sisal are also used to produce fabrics as an alternative to cotton.

Protein

Protein is essential to the structure and function of all living cells. The protein fibre keratin comes from hair fibres and is most commonly used in textile production.

Silk

Silk is derived from a protein fibre and is harvested from the cocoon of the silkworm. The cocoon is made from a continuous thread that is produced by the silkworm to wrap around itself for protection. Cultivated silk is stronger and has a finer appearance than silk harvested in the wild. During the production of cultivated silk the larva is killed, enabling the worker to collect the silk and unravel it in a continuous thread. Silkworms live off mulberry trees. For one kilogram of silk, around 100–200 grams of leaves must be eaten by the larva. Once extracted from the cocoon, the larva is often used as fish food by the farming community. In the wild, the silkworm chews its way out of its cocoon, thereby cutting into what would otherwise be a continuous thread. Silk fabric has good drape, handle and lustre.

2.4

Wool, cashmere, angora and mohair

Sheep produce wool fleece for protection against the elements, and this can be shorn at certain times of the year and spun into wool yarn. Different breeds of sheep produce different qualities of yarn; merino sheep produce the finest and most valuable wool. The majority of wool is produced in Australia and China.

Biodegradable and non-toxic pesticides are now more widely used in the production of wool to protect the sheep and improve the environment. Goats are also used to produce wool; certain breeds produce cashmere and angora. Cashmere is extremely soft and drapes well. Alpaca, camel and rabbit are also sources of fabrics with a warm, luxurious feel to them. Wool has a warm, slightly elastic quality, but it does not react well to excessive temperatures; when washed in hot water it shrinks due to the shortening of the fibres.

2.3 Mary Katrantzou
Digitally printed layered silk dress.

2.4 Christian Wijnants
Heavy hand-knitted jumper made from wool and angora.

Fur

Animals, such as mink, fox and finn raccoon, are bred on farms where the animals are purely reared for their skin. This subject causes heated debate between those for and against fur. The fur farmers would argue that the ethical treatment of the animals has always been an important part of the approach to fur farming. The quality of fur depends on the welfare of the animal; the higher the quality of life, the better the quality of fur.

Fur farmers in Scandinavia are regulated by national laws and guidelines, and regulations governed by the Council of Europe. Scientists work closely with the farmers and their research findings have already been adopted in areas such as housing, disease prevention, nutrition, husbandry, breeding and selection. The process of implementing other animal welfare measures as a result of scientific research is ongoing.

Anti-fur protesters would argue that some fur used in the clothing industry is used from animals 'caught' in the wild. The animals are trapped in snares or traps and undergo hours of suffering before they are brutally killed. As for 'farmed' fur, again, they would argue that the millions of animals killed every year are kept in small, cramped cages or enclosures. These living conditions go against the animal's natural instincts and cause severe stress, and can lead to cannibalism and self-mutilation. The killing process itself is not quick and painless. Methods including gassing, poisoning, electrocution, suffocation and neck breaking are commonplace.

2.5

2.5 Alexander Wang
The panels in this deconstructed leather coat are held together with a faggoting embroidery technique.

Hides and skins

Hides come from large animals such as cows, horses and buffalo, while skins are from smaller animals such as calves, sheep, goats and pigs.

Leather

Leather is made from animal skins or hides. The procedure used to treat the raw animal hides is called 'tanning'. Before this, the skins or hides are cured – a process that involves salting and drying – then they are soaked in water. This can take a few hours or a few days. The water helps to rid the skin of the salt from the curing process as well as dirt, debris and excess animal fats. Once the skins are free from hair, fat and debris, they are de-limed in a vat of acid. Next, the hides are treated with enzymes that smooth the grain and help to make them soft and flexible. The hides are now ready for the tanning process.

There are two ways of tanning – vegetable tanning and mineral tanning. The method used depends on the hide itself and the product intended. Vegetable tanning produces flexible, but stiff leathers that are used in luggage, furniture, belts, hats and harnesses. Mineral or chrome tanning is used on skins that will be used for softer leather products, such as purses, bags, shoes, gloves, jackets and sandals. The skins then go through dyeing and rolling processes, which dry and firm the leather.

The final step of the process involves finishing the skin. This is done by covering the grain surface with a chemical compound and then brushing it. Some leathers will show many imperfections after their final finishing, but they can be buffed or sandpapered to cover 'flaws'; after a period of prolonged buffing the leather becomes suede. 'Splitting' the leather can also produce suede, whereby the skin is cut into layers or splits with the outer or top layer being leather and then all the lower layers being suede. The higher-quality suede is in the upper layers.

Leather stretches but does not return to its original shape. DuPont has developed a fabric that is a fusion of leather and Lycra that has the properties of both. Napa is soft thin leather used for garments and can be made from leather skins or suede.

Metals

Fibres can be drawn from metal rods; alternatively, metal sheets can be cut into very fine strips. Metallic fibres can be used to decorate clothing. Traditionally, gold or silver strips were used, but they are fragile and expensive, and silver tends to tarnish. Nowadays, aluminium, steel, iron, nickel and cobalt-based superalloys are used.

Man-made fibres are made from cellulosic and non-cellulosic fibres. Cellulose is extracted from plants, as well as trees. Man-made fibres, such as rayon, Tencel, acetate, triacetate and lyocell, are cellulosic fibres as they contain natural cellulose. All other man-made fibres are non-cellulosic, which means they are made entirely from chemicals and are commonly known as 'synthetics'.

Developments in the chemical industry in the twentieth century caused a radical transformation in fabric production. Chemicals that had previously been used for textile finishing techniques began to be used to extract fibres from natural sources in order to make new fibres.

2.6 Man-made fabrics
Top row (left to right): spun rayon, Tencel/lyocell, nylon/elastane, nylon ripstop.
Middle row (left to right): silk/ viscose/spandex/velour, nylon fusing, viscose, satin viscose.
Bottom row (left to right): polyester, polyester wadding, metallic silk.

Cellulosic fibres

Cellulosic fibres are derived from cellulose, but through chemical manufacturing processes are developed into new fibres.

Rayon

Rayon was one of the first man-made fabrics to be developed. The first rayon dates back to 1885 and was called 'artificial silk' due to its properties. The name rayon was not established until 1924. As it is derived from cellulose (wood pulp), it has similar qualities to cotton in that it is strong, drapes well and has a soft handle. Rayon has excellent absorbency, so it is comfortable to wear and dyes well. Different chemicals and processes are used in the production of rayon, each with its own name. These include acetate rayon, cuprammonium rayon and viscose rayon, known commonly as 'viscose'. Lyocell and Modal are evolved from rayon.

2.7

Cellulose acetate

Cellulose acetate, more commonly known as 'acetate', was introduced during the First World War as a coating for aeroplane wings and was then developed into a fibre. It is made from wood pulp or cotton linters. Acetate shrinks with high heat and is thermoplastic, and it can be heat set with surface patterns such as *moiré*. It has the look, but not the handle, of silk. It does not absorb moisture well, but is fast to dry.

Tencel

Tencel was more recently developed to be the first environmentally friendly man-made fabric. It is made from sustainable wood plantations and the solvent used to extract it can be recycled, so the Tencel fibre is fully biodegradable. It produces a strong fabric that drapes like silk, with a soft handle.

2.7 Design by Rory Crichton
Rory Crichton's 'Strange I've seen that face before' textile design.

Non-cellulosic or synthetic fibres

Germany was the centre of the chemical industry until after the First World War when the USA took over its chemical patents and developed its inventions. DuPont was one of the large chemical companies developing fabrics at this time. In 1939, DuPont was able to produce long polymeric chains of molecules, the first being the polymer nylon. This was the beginning of the development of synthetic fabrics.

Most synthetics have similar properties. They are not particularly breathable, so many are not as comfortable to wear as natural fibres. They are sensitive to heat, so pleats and creases can be set permanently. The fabrics can also be glazed or embossed permanently. However, unwanted shrinkage and glazing can occur when a finished garment is pressed.

In general, synthetic fibres are white unless they are first dyed. Synthetic fabrics have poor absorbency, which means they dry quickly, but it makes them difficult to dye. Dyeing at the fibre stage of production produces a very colourfast fabric, but it means that the fabrics produced in this way cannot respond quickly to fashion trends, as the colour is determined early on in production.

Nylon

Nylon is a strong, lightweight fibre, but it melts easily at high temperatures. It is also a smooth fibre, which means dirt cannot cling easily to its surface. It has very low absorbency so dries quickly and does not need ironing. Nylon is made from non-renewable resources and is non-biodegradable.

During the Second World War, silk supplies from Japan were cut off, so the US government redirected the use of nylon in the manufacture of hosiery and lingerie to parachutes and tents for the military. Lycra is a form of nylon and was developed to use in lingerie, sportswear and swimwear.

Acrylic

DuPont developed acrylic in the 1940s. It has the look and handle of wool, but pilling can be a problem. It is non-allergenic, easy to wash, but sensitive to heat and melts under high temperatures.

Polyester

Polyester is a strong, crease-resistant fibre developed in 1941 by ICI. It is the most widely used synthetic fibre and is most commonly found in blends where it is used to reduce creasing, softening the handle of the cloth and adding drip-dry properties. Polyester was introduced to the USA as Dacron.

Polyester is made from chemicals extracted from crude oil or natural gas by non-renewable resources and the production of fibres uses large amounts of water for cooling. However, polyester can be seen as an environmentally friendly man-made fabric; if it is not blended, it can be melted down and recycled. It can also be made from recycled plastic bottles.

2.8

Spandex

Spandex is a super-stretch fibre as it can be stretched 100 per cent and will return to its original length. It was introduced by DuPont in 1959 and is a manufactured elastic fibre; it has similar properties to natural rubber, which is a natural elastic fibre. Spandex is used to add power stretch or comfort to textile products. Power stretch provides garments with holding power and is often used in underwear or swimsuits whereas comfort stretch adds only elasticity.

Aramid fibres

DuPont introduced aramid fibres under the trade name 'Nomex' nylon in 1963. The fibre is also known as 'Kevlar'. The fibres have exceptional strength and are five times stronger than steel. They are also flame resistant, decomposing at temperatures of about 371°C (700°F). Kevlar is used for strength applications where the fabric needs to be light, for example in bulletproof outfits. Nomex is used for its flame-resistance properties especially in military clothing and firefighting uniforms.

2.8 Vintage Comme des Garçons
The jacket is 100 per cent polyester with cotton panels and the skirt is 100 per cent polyester with velvet ribbon, lace and tape work.

Chemists are now producing fibres from natural sources, changing their structure to produce superior properties. They are also developing microfibres and nanotechnology, which can produce fabrics with advanced properties that can react to the environment in various ways.

Developments in the chemical industry in the twentieth century caused a radical transformation in fabric production. Chemicals that had previously been used for textile finishing techniques began to be used to extract fibres from natural sources in order to make new fibres.

2.9

2.9 Spider silk technology
Shown here is a brocaded shawl and cape. The shawl was made from the silk of more than one million female Madagascan golden orb-weaver spiders.

2.10 Marloes ten Bhömer
Shoe design by Marloes ten Bhömer incorporating a carbon fibre structure. The heels are positioned at the side of the shoe, making the wearer walk slightly differently, continuously moving the weight of the body from side to side.

2.10

Azlon

Azlon is a generic name for fibres regenerated from milk, peanut, corn and soybean proteins. Japan has produced a fibre made of milk protein and acrylic called 'Chinon'. It resembles silk and is used for garments.

Spider silk or BioSteel

Spider silk is naturally stronger than steel and is stretchy and waterproof. Biochemists are currently studying its structure and developing synthesized fibres with the same properties that could be used for fabric production. This new material is derived from protein in goat's milk and is trademarked BioSteel.

PLA fibre

This is a fibre that started being developed in 2001 under the trade name NatureWorks. It is derived from naturally occurring sugars in corn and sugar beet. The fibre is produced from a renewable source, needs little energy in production and is recyclable.

Odin Optim

Odin Optim is a fibre that has been developed by Nippon Keori Kaisha Ltd in Japan, the Woolmark Company and the Commonwealth Scientific and Industrial Research Organization (CSIRO). They have taken the wool fibre and altered its structure to produce a wool fabric that has superb drape and tactile qualities.

Microfibres

Microfibres are extremely fine fibres of one denier or less that have advanced properties. These fibres can be engineered into the construction of a fabric or can be used as a finishing coating.

Microfibre properties may include being lightweight, tactile, water-resistant, windproof or breathable, and they are often used in sportswear and high-performance clothing. As their properties are integral to the fibre, they will not wear or wash off.

The microfibre Tactel is produced by DuPont and has great tactile properties; there are different types of Tactel all with their own advanced properties. Microfibres can be expensive to manufacture so they are often mixed with cheaper fibres.

Microfibres can be produced with microcapsules that contain chemicals such as medication, vitamins, moisturizers, antibacterial agents, UV blockers or perfume. Chemicals in the microcapsules can be released onto the skin either by abrasion or as a result of heat given off by the body. Medication, vitamins or moisturizers can then be absorbed, imparting their benefits to the skin. However, these chemicals do get used up and gradually wash out of the fabric. Micro-organisms can also be incorporated that live off dirt and sweat, therefore maintaining cleaner, odour-free garments.

2.11–2.12 Microfibre technology
Anne Sofie Madsen has used microfibre-based fabrics in this collection. The synthetic fabrics give the collection a modern sportswear look.

Nanotechnology

Nanotechnology works at a molecular level, ultimately creating extremely intelligent and sophisticated fabrics that could be used in garments to change their colour, structure and even size. Currently, nanotechnology is used for producing finishings for fabric, for example Schoeller has developed a dirt-resistant coating for fabrics.

X-Static fabric

Metals can be woven into fabrics to make them more malleable and they are often mixed with synthetics for their anti-static properties. The use of silver is being developed within fabrics as a result of its antibacterial properties. X-Static, produced by Noble Biomaterials, bonds silver to the surface of another fibre to give it permanent antimicrobial properties, which are used to combat odours and athlete's foot.

Fibres

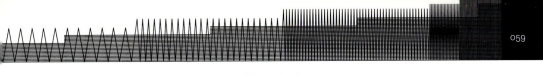

2.11   2.12

Most fibres go through a process that produces a yarn, which then goes through a construction process to produce a fabric. (Non-woven fabrics go from fibre straight to fabric – this will be discussed in the next chapter.)

The way in which a yarn is produced is related to the texture, functional properties, thickness and weight of the final fabric. Yarn producers will look to trend and colour predictions when producing and developing yarns to give aesthetic appeal as well as function.

2.13

2.13 Types of fibre
Shown anticlockwise (from top right): raw, unfinished sheep's wool fleece; spun wool; raw cotton (cleaned, but as grown from the plant); raw cotton (cleaned), carded and straightened; spun cotton yarn; elastane/lycra yarn; raw viscose rayon fibre (which is wood pulp dissolved and regenerated as viscose fibre); polyester yarn polymer chips melted and extruded as a continuous filament; linen yarn from flax plant; raw silk yarn spun from silk cocoons.

2.14

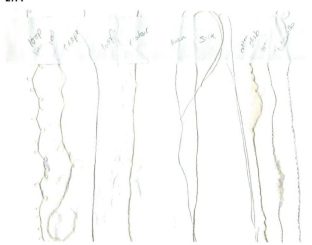

2.14 Types of yarn
Shown from left to right: linen loop; wool loop; crêpe; tape; mohair; linen; raw silk; silk; cotton slub; wool slub; chenille.

Yarn production

Fibres can basically be short, called 'staple fibres', or long and continuous, known as 'filament fibres'. During fibre production, synthetic fibres are put through a spinning process during which they are forced through small holes in a shower-head-style structure, creating long, continuous 'filament' fibres. Manufacturers can control the thickness of the fibre during this process. Filament fibres can be cut to resemble staple fibres, so mimicking the properties of natural fibres, synthetic fibres are cut down to become staple fibres when they are blended with natural fibres. All natural fibres are staple fibres excluding silk, which typically develops in a continuous length.

Spinning is also the name given to the process of twisting staple fibres together to make yarn. Yarn is twisted during the spinning process; the twist holds the short fibres together and contributes to strength. Yarn for weaving is tightly twisted to make it strong, while yarn for knitting is twisted more loosely to make it stretch. It also has better absorbency and a softer, warmer handle.

A single yarn is one yarn twisted, ply yarns are two or more single yarns twisted together. Two-ply yarn is two yarns twisted together and three-ply is three yarns twisted together. Ply yarns are stronger than single yarns.

Yarn can also be twisted and textured to enhance its performance or aesthetic qualities. Synthetic yarns can be heat set during manufacture to produce a texture.

Blending

Blending can occur during fibre production, yarn formation or in the processes of knitting and weaving. Yarns are blended to provide optimum qualities in a fabric. A blended yarn may drape and handle better. Blending can also add function or reduce the fabric cost. Synthetic fibres are often blended with natural fibres to improves their qualities, for example, polyester mixed with cotton produces a fabric that creases less.

Lycra and spandex can be mixed with other fibres to give stretch so that a fabric retains its shape; this is especially suitable for performance sportswear.

Types of yarn

Denier
Denier is the thickness of man-made fibres; the higher the denier, the thicker the fabric.

Cotton count
Cotton count is the numbering system for cotton yarns. The higher the number, the thinner the thread; sewing thread is normally 40.

Crêpe
Crêpe is highly twisted so that the yarn curls up, producing a crinkled surface in the finished fabric.

Bouclé
One yarn is wrapped around another yarn with a looser twist, which gives a pattern of loops, or curls, along its length. Fabric made from this yarn has a characteristically knobbly surface.

Slub
Slub has some parts of the yarn left untwisted.

Chenille yarn
Extra fibres are added into the twisted yarn to create chenille yarn.

Nepp
Nepp are small pieces of coloured fibres that are added to show up in the finished yarn.

The colour of a fabric can inspire, motivate and attract a designer or consumer to a particular article of clothing. There are also other aspects that can enhance a garment, such as a particular novelty dyeing effect or speciality coating that creates a look or feel that is unique and desirable. A dye is a colouring matter that works as a stain. It is absorbed into the fibres of a textile; the colour is not as easily worn away as a colour applied to the surface, such as pigment or paint.

Colour can be applied with synthetic or natural dyes at fibre, yarn, fabric or finished garment stages of production. If a garment is to be dyed, first test it for shrinkage; dyeing often requires high temperatures to fix the colour properly and the heat can cause the fibres to shrink. It is also important to make sure all the parts of the garment will react to the dye, for example the thread, zips, elastic and other trims. Fabric should be washed to remove any coatings before the dyeing process, as this will allow for better absorption. Remember that the original colour of the base cloth will affect the final dyed colour.

Natural, synthetic and man-made fabrics require specific dyes and fixers depending on their fibre type. Fabrics can be cross dyed for interesting effects. For example, fabrics composed of silk and viscose fibres could be dyed with acid and direct dyes, respectively. Most dyes can be used for printing fabric when mixed with a thickening agent.

2.15

2.15 Dye book
Dye sample swatches with their dye recipes have been carefully documented in this notebook for future reference.

2.16 Show piece from Alexander McQueen
Dye is sprayed onto this plain white dress creating a wonderful abstract design as the model rotates.

2.16

Natural dyes

Dyes originally came from soil, plants, insects and animals. For example, cochineal was obtained from the body of the female cochineal beetle and was used to produce red dye, while Tyrian blue was produced from shellfish. Some natural dyes produce a subtle colour, but their light and colourfastness are not as good as synthetic dyes. Natural dyes use renewable sources, however many need a huge amount of natural products to produce a small amount of dye. Also, many natural dyes need mordants to fix the colour and these can be harmful to the environment. There are two kinds of natural dyes: adjective and substantive.

Adjective dyes need a mordant to help the cloth to absorb the dye. The dye must form strong chemical bonds with the cloth to set the colour permanently. The mordant enters deeply into the fibre and when the dye is added, the dye and the mordant combine to form a colour; since the mordant is thoroughly embedded, so is the colour.

Substantive dyes do not need mordants during the dyeing process to make the fabric light and wash-fast. Indigo is the best known of these dyes.

2.17

2.18

Synthetic dyes

Towards the end of the nineteenth century, fabric manufacture expanded at a rapid pace due to the industrial revolution in Western Europe, predominantly in the UK. Great quantities of natural resources were needed to produce the dyes for the fabric. In some cases, the natural dyes were shipped from abroad, which was expensive and time consuming. As a result, chemists started to look at ways of producing synthetic 'copies' of natural dyes.

At this time, a purple dye called Tyrian purple was used to colour cloth worn by royalty; it was a difficult and expensive colour to produce as it was extracted from the mucus of molluscs. Fortunately, a young chemist named William Perkin accidentally invented the first synthetic purple dye, which was called 'aniline purple', or 'mauveine'. His discovery made him very wealthy and paved the way for the research and development of other synthetic dyes.

There are a wide variety of synthetic dyes formulated for different fabric types and for specific effects. Synthetic dyes tend to have a better light and wash fastness than natural dyes.

Basic dyes

Basic dyes were the first synthetic dyes to be developed, for example, Perkin's aniline dye. They have poor light and wash fastness and are not often used today except to dye acrylic fibres.

Mordants

Mordants prepare the fibre to receive the dyestuff and help the bonding. Most mordants come from minerals such as tin, chrome, alum (potassium alum), iron (ferrous sulphate) and tannin (tannic acid).

Natural mordants include mud, rushes, fungi, fruit peel and urine. The use of different mordants with the same dye can produce a variety of colours.

The water droplet test

Natural and synthetic fibres/fabrics contain impurities, such as oils and starches, and may also have been subjected to finishes applied during production, which can stop the successful absorption of dyes. A simple method for checking the purity of a fabric to be dyed involves applying a droplet of water to the surface. If it is quickly absorbed, there are no or few impurities or coatings on the fabric. If the water remains on the surface, the fabric will need to be washed before dyeing.

2.17–2.18 Viktor and Rolf
Half the collection was shown in black and the other half in shades of pink.

Acid dyes

The first synthetic dyes developed for wool were acid dyes. This class of dye has since grown into a large, diverse, versatile and widely used group. Some acid dyes may also be used for dyeing other protein fibres, including silk and also nylon or polyamide (at a higher temperature), which have a similar structure to protein fibres.

The term 'acid' refers to the fact that acid or an acid-producing compound is used in the dye bath. There are different types of acid dyes, including levelling and milling acid dyes. Levelling acid dyes are available in a range of bright colours and have good light fastness, but their wash fastness is only moderate. Milling acid dyes are also available in a range of bright colours and have good light and wash fastness, but are more difficult to apply correctly than levelling acid dyes.

Direct or substantive dyes

Direct or substantive dyes are suitable for dyeing cellulose fibres such as cotton and linen, but can also be used on silk, leather, wool and cellulose-mix fabrics. The first direct dye was called Congo red and was introduced in 1884. It was called a direct dye because it was the first dye to become available for colouring cellulose 'directly', without the use of a mordant.

However, the addition of common salt (sodium chloride) or Glauber's salt (sodium sulphate) improves the take up of dye. If wool or silk is dyed then acetic acid is added instead. Direct dyes are simple to use and come in a wide range of colours, albeit not very bright colours. The resulting dyed fabrics have poor wash fastness, so direct dyes are rarely used for printing.

2.19

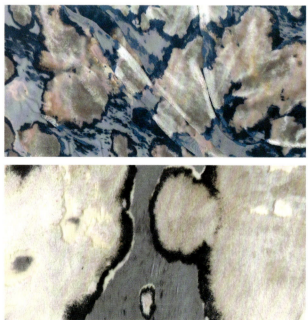

Dye classes

Different dyes are suitable for different fibres:

Acrylic
Basic, disperse (some).

Cellulose acetate
Disperse.

Cellulosic
Direct, reactive, vat, natural.

Nylon
Acid, disperse.

Polyamide
Acid, reactive (some).

Polyester
Disperse.

Wool
Acid, reactive (some).

Fibres

2.20

Disperse dyes

Disperse dyes were introduced in the 1920s to dye acetate fibres, which were otherwise unable to be dyed, with the notable exception of the natural dye logwood black, which was already being used on silk and wool. Nowadays, disperse dyes are mainly used for polyester fibres, but are suitable for most synthetic fibres. They are applied at relatively high temperatures so are not suitable for use on fabrics that are mixed with wool as the wool may felt. Disperse dyes have brilliant light-fast properties.

Reactive dyes

Developed in the 1950s, reactive dyes were the first dyes produced that chemically reacted with the fibre (usually cellulose) under alkaline conditions. The dye thereby becomes part of the fibre, rather than merely remaining an independent chemical entity within the fibre, which gives the fabric good wash and light fastness. Dyeing takes place in alkaline conditions normally through the addition of sodium carbonate. Common salt or Glauber's salt is also added, which helps the fabric take up the dye evenly. Variations in the amount of alkali and salt produces lighter or darker colours. Reactive dyes are suitable for dyeing cotton, linen and silk, and are often used for printing. These dyes were first marketed by ICI in 1956 as Procion dyes.

Pigments

Pigments are used for printing fabrics when mixed with the appropriate binder or thickening agent. They are easy to apply and do not need to be washed afterwards to remove the binder. This, however, means the printed area can be slightly stiff to handle.

Vat pigments

These are actually pigments that are insoluble in water. In order to apply them to fabric, they must first be subjected to a process of chemical reduction known as 'vatting', which makes them soluble. They can then be absorbed into the cloth. The fabric is then exposed to the air or treated with an oxidizing compound, whereby the reduced soluble form of the dye is reconverted to its original insoluble pigment form in the fibre, and so is not liable to be removed by washing.

Multipurpose dyes

Dyes produced for home use will dye most fabrics as they contain a mixture of dye types. They can be used in hot or cold water and some are ready to use in the washing machine.

**2.19–2.20 Print samples
by Mika Nash**
These samples have been created by first dyeing the *devoré* velvet with direct dischargeable dyes. Discharge paste is frozen into ice cubes then placed on the fabric and allowed to melt. When dried, the fabric is turned over and printed with *devoré* paste; the dye sets and also acts as a resist to the *devoré*.

Dyeing techniques can be used
to create pattern. Certain techniques
employ the use of resists that
are applied to the fabric and act
as a barrier to the dye. When the
fabric is dyed, the resist is then
removed and the fabric is left with
a negative pattern.

Tie-dye

Tie-dyeing involves tying twine around
areas of the fabric before dyeing; the twine
prevents dye from penetrating the cloth.
When the fabric is untied and dried, the areas
that have not been dyed form a pattern on
the fabric.

Fabric can also be stitched before it is
dyed. The stitches are pulled tight, which
creates areas where the dye cannot
penetrate, and gathered or folded first,
creating interesting effects.

Tie-dyeing has an interesting history as it has
been used since ancient times – the
Japanese call it 'shibori' and the craftspeople
of one region have developed numerous,
beautiful designs.

2.21

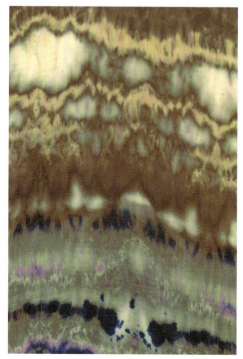

2.21–2.22 Tie-dye
Tie-dye textile samples designed by
Furphy Simpson.

2.23 Miu Miu
Coats in duchess satin have been
tie-dyed in the Miu Miu collection,
leaving them beautifully stained
and crumpled.

2.22

Fibres

2.23

Ikat

The warp or weft threads are tied with twine and then dyed, leaving a pattern where the twine was. When the warp or weft is woven into cloth it creates an *ombré* effect. A double ikat is produced when warp and weft are both dyed and woven together.

Colour testing

Companies test textiles under specific conditions for their colourfastness. The colour in swimwear must be fast to seawater and the chlorinated water found in swimming pools. Equally, a blouse worn next to the skin should not discolour as a result of perspiration. Because of the wide range of end uses for coloured textiles, many tests have been developed to assess fastness. Testing involves comparing a dyed sample that has been exposed to an agency, for example to light or to washing, with an original, to assess accurately any change in shade or change in depth of colour. Changes are accepted up to an agreed level depending on the end use of the dyed material, but if these levels are exceeded the product fails the test.

During washing, fastness testing, a coloured sample is tested with white fabric to assess the extent of staining. Fastness to light is, in fact, a measure of the ability of the dye molecule to absorb radiation without being destroyed. In a dye with poor light fastness, the molecule will be broken down by the absorbed radiation. No dye is completely fast to light, but it should not fade appreciably during the life of the article that it colours.

Starch and batik

Starch and wax working as a resist can be used to paint and draw designs onto fabric. The starch or wax is left to dry and the fabrics are dyed. The starch is then flaked off or with the wax-resist technique (batik), the fabric is boiled and the wax melts off.

Mechanical and chemical finishes can either take place at the fibre stage of the development of the fabric or on the actual finished surface of the textile. Processes can be used to add extra properties to a fabric or garment for visual, tactile or functional effect. Finishes can last the lifetime of a fabric or may wear off with time.

Basic finishes

These processes are necessary to prepare a fabric for dyeing or printing. Cleaning removes starch, dirt or grease after weaving or knitting. Desizing removes substances added to yarn before weaving to make the yarn stronger. Calico is not desized and, as a result, has a stiff handle. Scouring removes impurities from wool. Bleaching cleans and whitens manufactured fabric and can improve the dyeing process. During the stentering process, the fabric is pinned along its selvedge and stretched to realign the warp threads to their perpendicular position. You can see the pin marks down the selvedges of fabrics that have been stentered.

The milling process incorporates felting where moisture, heat and pressure are applied to fabrics causing wool fibres to contract and matt together. This process can be used to improve the handle of the cloth. The singeing process makes a fabric smoother as the fabric is passed over a flame and excess fibres are burnt off. Mercerization is usually used on cotton fabrics. Here, chemicals are added to the fabric that increase the fibre's lustre. It also makes the fabric stronger and more susceptible to dye.

Fabrics can be treated with optical brightening agents that are colourless fluorescent dyes; these react to UV light, making white fabric look whiter.

Aesthetic finishes

Aesthetic finishes help give a fabric the right feel or look. A fabric could have a high-tech finish added to it that makes it look more modern, or it may be that its finish could be a wash process that makes the fabric look older.

Putting a finish on a mixed-fibre fabric can create interesting effects as the fibres may react in different ways to the finish. For example, one fibre may shrink on heat, while the rest of the fabric remains static, therefore creating a crumpled or embossed surface. Chemical processes can change the tactile quality of the fabric, it may become soft and velvety or papery and dry to the touch.

Brushing the back of looped-back jersey sweatshirting will produce a fabric that now traps air and will insulate better.

During the calendering process, a fabric passes between heated rollers producing a flat glossy surface. A *moiré* finish can also be achieved using patterned rollers; the pressure and heat used produces a higher lustre.

2.24

Washing

Stonewashing was a hugely popular finish in the 1980s and was the fashion style of choice for numerous pop bands of that era. Stonewashing is achieved with the aid of pumice stones, which fade the fabric, but it is difficult to control and can damage the fabric and the machinery used to finish it. Acid dyes were introduced to perform the same task and the effects are called 'snow' or 'marble washes', but this type of process is not environmentally friendly.

Enzyme washes, or bio-stoning, are less harmful to the environment. Various effects can be achieved, depending on the mix and quantity of enzyme used within the wash. Enzyme washes can also be used to soften fabrics. Garments can be sand- or glass-blasted using a laser gun to target specific areas where fading and distressing is required. Lasers can also be used to produce precisely faded areas on a garment.

2.24 Lou Dalton
This jacket has been made from a coated cotton with a high sheen. Giving the outerwear in this collection by Lou Dalton a modern technical look.

Pleating

2.25

Washing can be used to give fabrics a creased or crinkled effect. Fabrics can be randomly creased by washing and leaving them unironed. Creasing and fixing the fabric before washing can form crinkles in specific areas. Permanent crinkles and pleats can be achieved on most synthetics and wool fabrics through applying heat and shaping as the fibres are permanently changed. This can also work on fabrics that are a high blend of synthetic. The hand-pleating process involves the fabric being placed between two already pleated textured cards; the cards are then rolled up and put into a steamer. The resulting fabric takes the texture of the pleated cards. The siroset process is used for wool and can be applied to specific areas of a garment to create a press line. A chemical is sprayed on to the front trouser leg and then steam pressed.

Issey Miyake signature pieces are made from thermoplastic polyester jersey. The garments are made first then pleated, which changes the garments' dimensions. As the garments are so stretchy due to the pleats, there is no need for zips or buttons. The flat construction of the garments has reference to the kimono.

Bacteria

Chemical treatments can also control the growth of bacteria on a fabric, thereby reducing odour. Teflon-coated fabrics also provide an invisible protective barrier against stains and dirt – useful for practical, easy-clean garments.

Performance finishes

Chemical and/or mechanical processes can alter a fabric for a functional process. Fabrics can be flameproof, stain repellent, anti-static, non-iron, moth- or mouldproof and can even be treated to reduce UV ray penetration. The use of new microfibres is being developed in this field. Fabrics can be waterproofed by applying a layer of rubber, polyvinyl chloride (PVC), polyurethane (PU) or wax over the surface. These fabrics are ideal for outdoor wear and footwear.

Reflective

Laminates applied to a textile give the cloth a new property and function. They can be visible or non-visible, while holographic laminates reflect and refract light.

Breathable

Breathable waterproof fabric is produced by applying a membrane to the surface that contains pores big enough to enable perspiration to escape from the body, but small enough to stop moisture droplets penetrating. GORE-TEX® is a superior example of this kind of fabric. The GORE-TEX® brand was first developed as light, efficient insulation for wire on Neil Armstrong's early space mission (Teflon is used to produce GORE-TEX®). It was then developed and registered as a breathable, waterproof and windproof fabric in 1976. It is now used widely for its properties in outerwear and sportswear.

Waterproofing

Natural oils left in the wool of a fisherman's jumper act as a naturally occurring waterproof layer. Fabrics can also be waterproofed by applying a layer of rubber, polyvinyl chloride (PVC), polyurethane (PU) or wax over the surface. These fabrics are ideal for outdoor wear and footwear.

2.25 Issey Miyake
This top has been cut very large then treated with a technique that heat sets in hundreds of tiny pleats to make the garment smaller and stretchy.

2.26 CP Company
Jacket using performance finished fabrication.

2.26

Manel Torres

What is your job title?
I am the managing director of Fabrican Limited.

Please describe your job.
My job is to provide the creative leadership for Fabrican. I am responsible for its direction and strategy, as well as the commercial and financial management of the company.

What was your career path to your current job?
I see my career path as a journey from my childhood in Catalonia, Spain, to London, and then onwards to working with Fabrican's partners, who can now be found across the world from North America to Japan.

I studied at the Royal College of Art in London, UK. I completed my PhD with the collaboration of the Royal College and Imperial College, UK. This gave me the tools, knowledge and creative inspiration to make my dreams a reality. Now, I find myself at the heart of the 'Albertopolis' in London, 'the square mile of knowledge' where the Royal College of Art and Imperial College are both located along with some of the world's most famous museums and galleries.

What do you do on an average day?
My days are unpredictable and usually very long. They are taken up with meeting visitors and discussing our ongoing projects. There are hundreds of enquiries about Fabrican from all over the world every week, which we do our best to respond to.

I frequently need to travel to international conferences or to meet our development partners, and I am also asked to appear on many television or radio programmes. There are many dinners to attend. At the end of the day I am usually happy, but very tired!

What are the essential qualities needed for your job?
I believe the essential qualities needed for my job are to be single minded in my vision, but also to communicate this effectively to motivate others.

How creative a job do you have?
It is extremely creative, and I have learned how creative the scientific and business world can be compared to what we regard as the traditional creative industries. Every day our goal is to create something new and do things in a way that they haven't been done before.

You are developing a product rather than a fashion collection – how different is this process?
In terms of the mental approach, they are very similar. You need an idea and the creative vision. You must apply the same meticulous care and technical skill in the realization. Some of the tools are different, but the same care, skill and professionalism apply. I have always been surprised at how natural the relationship between science and the arts is, and frustrated by the artificial barriers that have been built up between them.

What is more important to your future work: innovation or sustainability?
The two are inextricably linked, and for Fabrican they have a symbiotic relationship. The great thing about the spray-on fabric is that it is both reusable and can be instantly recycled. Our remaining challenge is to become truly resource neutral. Imagine that!

What do you think you will be doing in ten years' time?
New ideas, new technology, new challenges. Not knowing exactly what these will be is the most exciting thing!

What advice would you give someone wanting a job in your area of design?
You need patience, hard work and consideration for the people around you. You have to be true to your own ideals, but check that other people are also inspired by your ideas; otherwise, you may be very lonely!

2.27 Manel Torres
Sprayed fabric 'Rose' dress.

2.27

From this chapter you now understand that fabric is made from a fibre taken from natural or synthetic sources. The fibre is then made into a yarn for weaving or knitting, or it can used to create a fibre in other ways, such as pouring or bonding. After construction, a fabric can be finished in various ways for function or decorative effect, for example to create a waterproof fabric or dyed into a vivid fashionable colour.

In this project, we create innovative new textiles by experimenting with finishing techniques.

You will try to produce something new from something old and wherever possible try not to spend any money.

Please be careful as some of the processes could be dangerous; wear protective clothing, use gloves and protect your eyes.

2.28 Sophie Copage leather design
The pattern on the leather is achieved through the application of heat.

Project A: Coating fabrics

Continuing from the last chapter's project, take some of the samples you created (you may need to supplement these with other fabrics that you find around your home from old garments). Follow the steps below to create new experimental coated samples.

Step 1: Try rubbing wax over the surface of a sample; this could produce a waterproof finish or just an interesting shiny or matt effect. You could use a stencil so certain areas are left untreated.

Step 2: Liquid latex can be painted or poured onto a fabric's surface; the latex can be coloured or things can be trapped in the fluid when drying.

Project B: Deconstructing/ageing

It is interesting to see how we can age or deconstruct a fabric. Denims undergo various ageing techniques during production, the simplest of which is a pumice stonewash. A distressed look can be applied to the whole garment or just certain areas such as knees, elbows and seams.

Step 1: To make a fabric look worn, try rubbing a pumice stone or sandpaper over the surface, or scoring it with a razor blade. Be careful not to destroy the fabric's structure too much as it will rip or fall apart. Try different pressures and movements for experimental effect.

Step 2: In 1993, the fashion designer Hussein Chalayan buried a number of silk dresses from his graduate collection with iron fillings in his back garden for several weeks to see how they would decompose and age.

2.28

Resist effects can be created with bleach. Take a fabric and pleat it up like a fan then tie string around the pleats covering about two centimetres of fabric, repeat at an interval of five centimetres. Now drop this into a pan of cold bleach mixed with water. When you take out the fabric, wash it and then remove the string. You will have created a bleached pattern; this can look great on a printed fabric.

Step 2: Dyeing fabric with natural materials will produce more subtle effects than shop-bought dyes. It really is a case of experimentation – try different materials, different mordants, various dyeing times and quantities of water. Write down your processes and attach a swatch of the dyed fabric as a record.

You could try the same thing yourself, or see what happens if you leave a rusty object in water with fabric.

Step 3: Designer Sophie Copage used a soldering iron to draw on the back of leather to beautiful effect. The skin shrinks and puckers where the heat touches it. A hair dryer or iron would scold or shrink leather or a synthetic fabric; placing a stencil on first to block some heat could create an interesting effect (be careful not to burn yourself).

Natural fabrics, such as wool and silk, are better at dyeing naturally than synthetic fabrics. Not all dyestuff need a mordant, but some will need a fixative for the dye to take to the fabric. Easy mordants to find are vinegar or salt. Start by washing your fabric to help remove any finish it might have that could prevent the dye taking up. Next, put the fabric with the mordant in water and bring to a simmer (try various times for different results, maybe 15 minutes or an hour).

Project C: Colouring

Colouring a fabric can dramatically change its appearance. Try over-dyeing or bleaching a patterned fabric, or maybe treating just part of the fabric sample. Using a resist, in the form of wax, string or elastic bands, can create patterns.

Step 1: Bleach can produce various results depending on how strong it is or with what it is mixed (be careful with bleach; wear gloves and protect your eyes).

Next, take your dyestuff, for example onion, tea, coffee, turmeric, berries, roots or mud, and either lightly crush or dissolve the natural material in a pan of water. The material could then be soaked overnight and then brought to the boil and simmered for an hour (again try different times), or it could be heated without the initial soak. You are then ready to put your fabric into the pan and leave to dye.

3

In order to transform lengths of yarn into fabric to wear, the yarn must go through a process of construction: the two main fabric constructions are knit and weave. Other types of construction include crochet, lacemaking and macramé. Fabric can also be made directly from fibres and solutions. Tyvek is made from the matting together of fibres to make a paper-like fabric. Mass-produced shoulder pads are made from foam that comes from a solution. Leather and fur are probably the oldest types of 'fabric' that have been used by humans to clothe themselves. They are not constructed, but are cut from the animal as a skin.

When looking at fabric construction it is important to consider what properties a certain technique will give to a fabric, and ultimately the finished garment.

A knitted fabric will tend to be used for its comfort, stretch and ease of fit. A woven fabric may be used when a garment needs structure and stability, whereas a lacy fabric could be used for its decorative qualities. However, a knitted fabric can be structural if knitted and then felted. A woven fabric can be stretchy and comfortable if woven with Lycra and can also be decorative if produced on a jacquard loom.

Fabric Construction

3.1 Jessica Leclère
In this garment Leclère has woven strips of wood into the knit.

3.1

A woven fabric is made from a warp that runs down the length of a fabric and a weft that weaves across the breadth of the fabric. The warp and weft are also known as the 'grain'. If the grain is not at 90°, the fabric is said to be 'off grain' and may not hang or drape properly, which can cause problems when making up a garment. The warp is stretched onto a loom before weaving; this means there is more 'give' across the width of the fabric where the weft is woven across. The warp is sometimes coated with starches to increase the strength of the yarn; these starches are washed out in a finishing process when the fabric is woven.

The loom traditionally had a shuttle carrying yarn back and forth under and over the warp yarns. This process can still be seen in today's production methods.

Newer shuttleless looms use air or water jets to propel the weft yarn across the warp at incredibly fast speeds. These machines are a lot quieter than traditional looms. The weft yarn is not continuous, but is cut to length before it is passed across the warps. Looms can be circular, producing a tube of fabric, and also double-width, producing two widths of fabric at the same time – denim is often woven in this way. The way the warp and weft are woven together produces a variety of fabrics. The three main types of weave construction are plain, twill and satin.

Plain weave fabrics

Calico
Calico is plain cotton fabric that has not gone through a finishing process. It therefore still contains starch from weaving and has a slightly stiff handle.

Canvas
A heavy weight tightly woven cotton fabric.

Chambray
Chambray is a medium weight fabric with white warp yarns and coloured weft yarns of cotton or cotton-mix origin.

Chiffon
Chiffon is a lightweight soft fabric.

Gingham
Gingham features a small check weave structure usually made up of two colours.

Muslin
Muslin is a lightweight soft-handled plain weave, usually white or unbleached cotton.

Organdy
Organdy is a sheer, crisp lightweight cotton.

Organza
Organza is a sheer, crisp, lightweight cotton made from filament yarns, for example, silk or synthetic yarns.

Voile
Voile is a lightweight fabric made with two-ply warp in cotton, cotton mixes or man-made fibres.

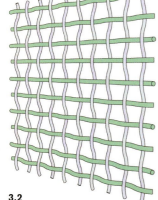

3.2 Plain weave
Diagram showing a basic warp and weave structure

3.3 Plain weave structures
Shown left column
(top to bottom):
rib, basket weave waffle; plain weave, plain weave with chintz.
Middle column (top to bottom):
chiffon, silk organza, georgette, cotton voile.
Right column (top to bottom):
gingham, chambray, canvas, seersucker.

3.3

Plain weave

Plain weave is constructed from a warp
and weft that is similar in size. During the
weaving process, the weft is passed over
alternate warp threads to create the fabric
and is usually closely woven. Basic plain
weaves have a flat characteristic and are
good for printing and techniques like pleating
and smocking. Using different yarn weights
and tensions creates variations to the
plain weave.

Also, the chemicals used are absorbed by the
cotton plant and remain in the cotton during
manufacture, which means that it is still in the
fabric that we wear next to our skin. Due to
these issues, manufacturers are increasingly
developing organic fibres that are grown and
processed without the use of artificial
fertilizers and pesticides. Organic fabric
production is more expensive, but it has a low
impact on the environment and is healthier
for the consumer. There are designers
pursuing organic solutions, such as Katharine
Hamnett and Edun (also see page 25).

Structure variations

There are many variations in the
structure of plain-weave fabrics:

Ribbed
Ribbed fabric is created by
grouping warp or weft yarns or
using thicker yarns in areas of
the cloth.

Basket weave
Basket weave is a loosely woven
fabric achieved by alternately
passing a weft under and over a
group of warps so the weft lies
over the warps. This is repeated
to produce a square pattern in
the fabric.

Seersucker
With seersucker fabric the warp
is held at different tensions, one
set of warp yarns is held tight
with the remaining yarns held
slack. As the weft is inserted
across the warp, a puckered
effect is created by the looser
warp yarns.

3.4

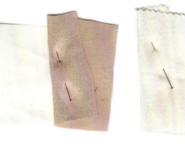

Twill weave fabrics

Chino
Chino has a steep twill and is made from combed or two-ply yarns.

Denim
Denim is usually made from yarn-dyed cotton or cotton blends.

Drill
Drill is a dyed medium weight or heavy weight fabric.

Herringbone
Herringbone is an even-sided twill where the wale regularly reverses to form a chevron pattern.

Tweed and houndstooth
Tweed and houndstooth are twills using different coloured yarns and weave structures to create pattern.

Twill weave

During the twill weave process, the weft is woven over at least two warp threads before it goes under one or more warp threads. Where this is staggered down the length of the fabric it produces diagonal lines on the surface of the fabric; these lines are called 'wales'. The wale can run at various degrees across the fabric; a regular twill runs at a 45° angle, while a steep twill runs at more than 45°. Twill lines or wales can also run from left to right – a right-hand twill, or right to left – a left-hand twill.

3.4 Twill and satin weaves
Shown top row (left to right): silk cotton twill, twill, cotton gabardine, drill. Middle row (left to right): denim, tweed, herringbone, houndstooth. Bottom row (left to right): polyester satin, silk satin, cotton sateen.

3.5 Silk satin
Peter Jensen silk satin top incorporating pearl necklace detail.

3.5

Double-faced satin
The front and back have a smooth satin line finish as the fabric is woven with two warps and one weft.

Crêpe-back satin
The fabric is woven with a high-twist crêpe yarn that shows on the back, and a lower twist yarn that shows a smooth satin finish on the front.

Sateen fabrics
Sateen fabrics are made from spun yarns, usually cotton.

Satin fabrics
These are often made from filament yarns with low twist.

Tweed and houndstooth
Tweed and houndstooth are twills using different coloured yarns and weave structures to create pattern.

Wales can show on one side of the fabric or can show equally on the front and back of the fabric. Twills are usually closely woven and are strong and hard-wearing fabrics.

Satin weave

Satin weave has visible sheen and feels smooth due to a tightly woven weave structure that allows yarn to lay across the surface of the fabric. The warp is woven to lie on top of the weft or vice versa. Satin weave fabrics are often used for lining as they glide easily over other garments.

The three basic weave structures can be varied to produce more complicated weave structures.

Double cloth

Double cloth is the result of weaving two interconnected cloths at the same time. Velvet is commonly woven as a double cloth – that is, cut apart after weaving to produce two fabrics that are the same. Double cloth construction can also produce a fabric made of two quite different qualities, patterns or colours. This kind of fabric is reversible so that either side can be used as the outer layer of a garment. Sometimes, the fabric is connected all over or it may be just connected in some parts creating pockets and puckers.

Pile fabrics

Pile fabrics are woven with extra yarns to the basic warp and weft, which create floats or loops that can then be cut, for example corduroy, or left as loops, as in towelling.

Double-cloth fabrics

Melton
Usually wool produced in the double-cloth process, but not cut through afterwards, which produces a heavy fabric suitable for outerwear.

Velour
A woven fabric or felt resembling velvet. Produced using the same process as velvet construction, but usually made from cotton yarn.

3.6 Other weave structures
Shown left column (top to bottom): silk, velvet, cotton velvet, jumbo cord, needle cord.
Middle column (top to bottom): ripstop dobby patterns, cotton spot weave with cut threads, wool double cloth.
Right column (top to bottom): jaquard, moleskin, resin-coated cotton, crêpe.

Engineered weave

It is interesting to consider engineering pattern, colour or function in a weave. An elastic yarn could be woven across the width of a fabric to change its construction. The elastic would constrict when released, bringing the fabric in. This could then be cut and incorporated into a garment that when placed on the body would tighten to fit in specific areas. Computer-aided weave can produce fabrics with many layers and surfaces. In jean production, sometimes the denim is woven narrowly so that the selvedge edge can be incorporated into the trouser leg. It is the finished edge to the inside seam.

Shape-memory alloys, such as nickel and titanium, can be woven into fabrics so that the fabric regains its shape with the application of a certain temperature. This principle is used in the production of bras; the wire in the cup retains its shape and bra structure when the bra is put through the washing machine.

Pile fabrics that show pattern

Corduroy
Extra weft yarn is woven leaving regular floats, which are cut and brushed up to form piled lines working down the fabric that can be of varying thickness. Fine lines are known as 'needle cord', large lines as 'jumbo cord'.

Towelling
Towelling is created by slack tension weaving, which creates loops on the surface of the cloth in a similar way to the construction of seersucker, as discussed earlier.

Velveteen
A fabric with an all-over cut pile, usually made from spun yarns.

Other weave structures

Brocade
Brocade uses different coloured yarns to produce a highly patterned fabric with many floats on a plain, satin or twill base.

Damask
Damask is usually constructed in one or two colours in a similar way to brocade.

Jacquard
Creates patterns and textures through a complicated weave system in which warp and weft threads are lifted or left. Often, long floats occur on the fabric that can catch and snag.

Dobby
These weaves have small repeated geometric patterns in their structure.

Pique
The dobby weave is used to create a surface pattern.

Spot weaving
Yarns are added to the basic warp and weft to create pattern and texture in places.

Waffle
A dobby weave that produces a honeycomb pattern.

Knitting dates back to the Egyptians, but was really developed into an industry in Europe in the early sixteenth century. Knitting machines were developed in the second half of the eighteenth century due to the demand for patterned stockings; and following the invention of the rotary knitting machine, tubular knitting could be produced for hosiery.

In the nineteenth century, British sailors and fishermen developed styles of knitting that incorporated pattern and texture that are still well known today. Fishermen's Guernseys or 'ganseys' originated in the Channel Islands in Guernsey, and at one point a fisherman's region of origin could be identified by the pattern of his Guernsey. Texture was important, often incorporating cables that looked rather like the fishermen's ropes. An Aran knit was originally cream and heavily embossed with cable, honeycomb, diamond and lattice patterns. The patterns were handed down from generation to generation often just visually rather than being written down as a pattern.

Fair Isle is a term that is used to describe patterned knitting in multicolours. It should, however, really be used to describe the specialized colours and patterns used in Shetland knitting; Fair Isle is an island south of Shetland. Shetland is positioned between Scotland and Norway and the influence of a folk-style motif is apparent in Fair Isle patterns; the motifs tend to work in bands on the knit and are not random. Shetland sheep produce fine soft-quality wool that is not clipped from the sheep, but plucked by hand.

The wool is available in a variety of colours such as white, cream, fawn, grey and black. The wool is also dyed with lichens to achieve soft rose, pale yellow and purplish browns.

Patterns from other European countries tend to be more bold and graphic than British designs. The Bjarbo pattern from Sweden was traditionally worked in red and blue on a cream background. Scandinavian designs also use small figures on a light background and an eight-pointed star was common in Norwegian designs.

In the late nineteenth and early twentieth centuries, fashions changed and women and men began wearing jumpers and cardigans and other knitted garments for day, evening and, more importantly, for sports. With the increase in leisure time, knitted fabric has become increasingly important for sportswear as it is stretchy, comfortable and absorbent.

Fabric Construction

3.7 Johan Ku
'Re-sculpture' collection
Design incorporating machine knit
and hand crochet techniques.

Knitted fabrics

Knitted fabrics are constructed from interconnecting loops of lengths of yarn, which can be knitted along the warp or weft, giving the fabric its stretchy quality. Horizontal rows of knit are known as 'courses' and vertical rows are known as 'wales'. Weft knitting is created from one yarn that loops and links along the course; if a stitch is dropped, the knit is likely to ladder and run down the length of the wale. Hand knitting is a prime example.

Warp knitting is more like weaving, with the construction being more complicated and the fabric less easy to unravel. Knitted fabric tends to be comfortable to wear as it is stretchy, but this can also mean that it can stretch out of shape and shrink with heat, especially if it is made from wool.

Knitted fabrics tend to be more prone to pilling than woven fabrics. This is because loosely spun yarns are often used for knitted construction and these pill more than tightly spun yarns. Different thicknesses of knitting can be produced according to the stitch used, the size of the needles and the thickness or the count of the yarn. Knit finishes can change the quality of the fabric. For example, softeners can be used to improve the handle of the cloth. Washing at a high temperature and using friction can cause woollen knit to felt, which in turn causes the fibres to matt together, making the knit denser and less stretchy.

3.8

3.8 Sonia Rykiel sketch and knit swatches
The inspiration for this piece was vintage underwear.

3.9

Basic stitches

Texture and pattern can be created by knitting with different needles, yarns, colours or stitches. Stitches add decorative quality, but they can also benefit the physical quality of a knit, for example the use of tuck stitch or cable increases the density of the fabric. It is important how the swatch looks, but also how it feels and how it drapes. Experiment with stitches, techniques and tensions to create something unique. Knit can be embroidered to highlight areas and beads can be inserted into stitches for a more decorative effect.

Slip or float stitch

These can be used to create patterns or change colour within a piece of knitting. The yarn is stitched then floats across the back of the fabric before it is used again. It is best not to allow the floats to be too long as they tend to catch and cause snagging. These floats also restrict the stretch of the fabric and make the finished knit heavier. Fair Isle and jacquard incorporate this method to create pattern. The wrong side of the fabric can be used as the right side and the floats can be cut, for textural decorative effect. On modern automatic machines, the floats are knitted in on a jacquard pattern to produce a double-sided knit.

3.10

Intarsia

Here, pattern is created with yarn changes, but the yarn does not travel across the back of the fabric creating floats, which means that larger colour blocks can be used in a design.

3.9 Winni Lok
This Winni Lok knitted sweater uses the right side of the fabric on the front of the jumper, and the wrong side with floats on the back.

3.10 Sonya Rykiel
Vintage Sonya Rykiel merino wool intarsia pattern jumper.

Tuck stitch

The stitch is held on the needle as the rest of the piece continues to be knitted, creating a pulled or tucked effect. Small honeycomb patterns to larger bubbled or puckered effects can be created, and both sides of the fabric can be used showing either a bubbled look or indent.

Lace stitch or stitch transfer

A stitch is transferred to another needle, creating a hole as the knitting continues. Single stitches or groups of stitches can be transferred from needles by hand using a transfer tool to create interesting patterns. Lace knitting has been produced in Europe since the fifteenth century, but did not become popular until the eighteenth century when fine cotton was imported from the East. It was known as 'white knitting' as the yarn used was predominantly undyed. Laddering effects can be created through transferring stitches creating large controlled holes in the knit.

Partial knitting

Needles are selected so some stitches are knitted and others are held on the needles. This is used for decorative effects and also for shaping garments for a dart or flare.

Cable knit

Stitches are transferred across a knit, therefore creating raised twisted groups of stitches. Cables are used more commonly in hand knitting as raised three-dimensional designs can be created; however, they can also be created on the V-bed machine. Wool yarn is good for this technique as it is elastic and will allow stitches to stretch during transfer.

Inlay

A yarn is woven or laid onto the knit and the stitches catch it down. The laid yarn does not create loops as normal knitting does, so it tends to make the knitted fabric less stretchy. Yarns that would normally be too thick, thin or maybe too textured to knit with, can be successfully incorporated into the knit using this method. Fringing and looping can also be incorporated in this way to the knit.

3.11 Xavier Brisoux
Neck detail showing partial knitting and floats.

3.12 Vintage Tao
Comme des Garçons
100% polyester machine knit featuring a tuck effect to create a blistered pattern.

3.13 Marc by Marc Jacobs
Sweater featuring owl motifs knitted using a cable stitch.

3.11

3.12

3.13

3.14

Machine knitting

Originally, knitting was produced by hand, but this developed into machine knitting for mass production. Fabrics can be knitted flat or as a circular tube, with each needle producing a column of stitches (wale) in the fabric.

Machines that work with fine to medium yarn are known as 'fine gauge' with 250 needles across the bed. A standard gauge contains 200 needles; a chunky gauge contains 100 needles and is ideal for thicker yarns.

It is important not to use a yarn that is too thick for the capacity of the machine, otherwise it will jam the machine or the yarn will snap. A thicker yarn could instead be laid into a design. Certain yarns that are darker may knit in a different way to paler yarns as the dye alters the properties, making them less elastic.

Wool is one of the best yarns to knit with as it recovers its shape well after stretching or distorting. In contrast, cotton can be hard to knit with due to its inelastic quality and it is more liable to break.

Single-bed machines

Single-bed machines have one flat bed of needles all working in the same direction producing stocking stitch.

Single-jersey knit has a front 'knit' and a back 'purl', and is produced when using one bed of needles. This fabric can be heavy- or lightweight, can ladder and run, and tends to curl when cut. Sweatshirting is a heavier knit, the back of which is looped or brushed to achieve a fleeced effect.

Punch cards are used on domestic machines to select needles more quickly than by hand in order to create pattern and texture. The card is fed into the machine and row-by-row selects needle positions. Pre-punched cards can be bought, or cards can be punched for specific designs.

Computer-linked jacquard and knitting machines can produce very intricately patterned fabrics from drawings and photographs through complicated needle selection, and designs can also be worked across a large area. The use of CAD also allows knitting designs to be changed quickly and respond to fashion trends.

Shaping aids are used with domestic machines to allow the knitter to quickly and simply create shaped knitting without having to manually count stitches and rows.

3.14 Knitting machine
Single-bed domestic
knitting machine.

3.15 Leutton Postle
This dress has been machine-knitted with laid in yarns that add colour and texture.

3.15

Double-bed machines

Double-bed or V-bed machines have two sets of needles set opposite each other and produce double-knit or rib fabric. A double bed can be created on a domestic single bed by attaching a ribber. Dubied is a brand of an industrial hand-operated double-bed machine. They produce a good quality of knit, but the machines are very expensive and very heavy.

Interlock knit or double jersey is produced with a double row of needles and the knit looks the same front and back, showing a knit stitch, or a 1x1 rib on both. Ribs and other textured knitting are also produced using two beds of needles knitting alternate knit and purl stitches. Ribs can be used to finish garments on the cuffs or waistband where a garment needs to be gathered in. Due to their construction, they have greater stretch. Ribs can also be used to produce a whole garment. A 2x2 rib has two columns of knit stitches and then two columns of purl stitches alternating across the fabric; 3x3 would have the corresponding number of stitches and so on. Rib knits are more elastic than single-jersey knits.

Electronic industrial machines

Some industrial machines have four-needle beds, which allow for more shaping, colour changes and yarn changes. Sophisticated machines can also knit and construct garments with little or no seams. Circular machines produce a tube of knitting. They are very fast as they continuously knit, and one row can be started before the last row has finished. The fabric, however, can twist due to the manufacturing process. If a flat piece of fabric is needed, the tube is then cut through and the edges sealed before being processed as it has no selvedge and would otherwise run. Examples of electronic knitting machines are Stoll, Shima Seiki and Protti.

Warp knitting machines

Warp knits are usually created on a flat knitting machine and this is the fastest way to produce fabric from yarn. The main makes of machine are Tricot or Raschel. Tricot knits tend to use fine yarns and produce smooth, simple fabrics, whereas Raschel knits are more textured and have open work designs in heavier yarns. Fine nets, laces and powernet fabrics are produced on a Raschel machine. New research in warp knitting has resulted in the creation of seamless garments. Issey Miyake is known for his A-POC (a piece of cloth) tubular clothing where garment shapes are cut out of a knitted tube length, each garment featuring cut lines that when cut do not run or ladder. The wearer interacts with the garment and can customize it using the cut lines to their specific requirement.

3.16 Nanna van Blaaderen
Chunky hand knit featuring a large twisted cable in a thick, soft merino wool.

3.17 Industrial knitting machine
Circular knitting machine used for mass production.

Fabric Construction

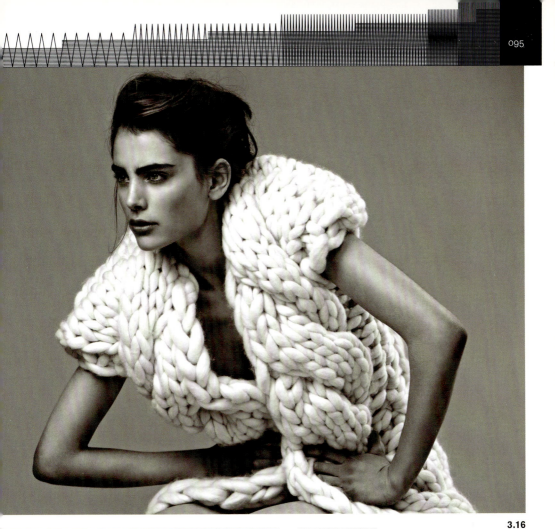

3.16

Hand knitting

Hand knitting can produce a variety of weights of fabric and has its own 'home-made' character; it is especially suited to very heavy knits and cables. It is possible to create a fabric very quickly with thick yarns and large needles. It is also a very transportable means of constructing a fabric as it can be carried around and worked on in any location.

3.17

There are many other fabric constructions other than knit and weave, and they can be used to produce a variety of fabrics ranging from decorative, handcrafted looks to functional and technologically advanced creations.

3.18

3.19

Types of lace

Alençon
A needlepoint lace. A fine corded pattern worked on a mesh background.

Chantilly
A very delicate intricate lace often featuring flowers or vines.

Cluny
French bobbin lace.

Rose point
A needlepoint lace with elaborate raised patterns.

Knotted and twisted

These techniques have a handcrafted look and involve yarns that are twisted and knotted together to produce fabrics that are decorative and have an open structure.

Crochet

The word crochet comes from the French word *croc,* meaning 'hook'. Stitches are made using a single hook to pull one or more loops through previous loops of a chain. This construction can be built up to form a patterned fabric. Different from knitting, crochet is composed entirely of loops made secure only when the free end of the strand is pulled through the final loop. Crochet hooks vary in size so they can be used to produce different structures of fabric. Fine needles and yarn create a lacy fabric, while thicker needles and hooks create a more solid fabric. Textures can be created by either wrapping yarn around the hook before it is stitched or by working stitches on top of existing stitches. More open-work fabric with holes and spaces can be created by forming bars and lines of stitches. Fabrics can also be made by building up rows of stitches or from working in the round, from a circle out.

Macramé

Macramé is constructed through the ornamental knotting of yarn, giving the fabric a hand-crafted appearance.

Lace

Lacemaking produces a fabric that is light and open in structure. The negative holes in lace are as important as the positive stitches in the overall pattern of the fabric.

Needlepoint lace is based on embroidery techniques, and bobbin lace is based on braiding techniques. They were both developed in the late sixteenth century and were the most expensive type of ornamentation at the time. In Europe, lace production mainly came from Italy, France and Belgium, and the lace was named after the region it was produced in. Irish crochet lace originated from the Italian needlepoint lace of the seventeenth century, and from the nineteenth century, Ireland became the main producer. Lace became very popular again in the early twentieth century, with patterns often depicting organic shapes and insects in the art nouveau style.

Originally, lace was made by hand, but now it is mainly produced using the Levers machine. Lacy knits can be created on Raschel knitting machines and lacy embroideries can be produced using the Schiffli embroidery machine.

3.18 Macramé
Eleanor Amoroso has hand macraméd this dress.

3.19 Crochet
Laura Theiss created crochet panels that were then placed on the stand and stitched together to form this dress.

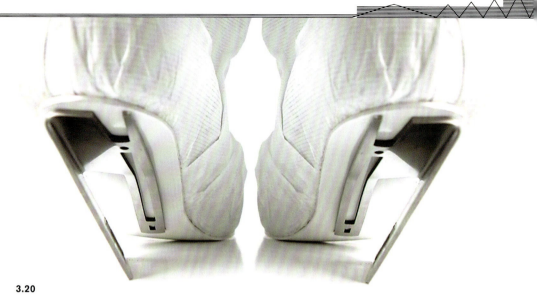

3.20

Non-woven constructions

Non-woven fabrics can be used for fashion garments, but are also used for linings, padding and the interiors of shoes and bags. Due to their construction, non-woven fabrics have no grain and do not fray or unravel in the same way as woven fabrics, which makes them eminently more suitable for garments or accessories that need to be more hard-working and reliable. Other non-wovens are being developed for future fabrics.

Chemical and mechanical

Compressing fibres together with the use of heat, friction or chemicals can produce fabrics. Examples of this are felt, rubber sheeting and Tyvek. Tyvek, produced by DuPont, is made by matting fibres together – almost like the way paper is made. It also has a coating that makes it tear-proof, water-resistant, recyclable and machine washable. Fabrics can also be made from solutions; foams and films are examples of this.

3.20 Tyvek, leather and stainless steel slip-on boots by Marloes ten Bhömer
These boots look into the aesthetics of destruction, in order to create a new silhouette form. The front of the boot is distorted and dented. Normally a slip-on boot is very straight at the back so your foot can slide into the boot. The way the patterns have been cut enables the back of the boot to hug the calf and leg.

Fabric Construction

3.21

Sprayed fabric

Manel Torres has developed a way of producing a textile by literally spraying the fibres from a can; in this way, a fabric can be sprayed directly onto the body. Areas can be built up to be thicker than others and there is no need for fastenings as the garment is cut off at the end of its use. The fabric adheres to the form of the body. If a shape is needed, moulds can be placed underneath to shape the garment. In this way, Torres is combining design with chemistry.

3D forming

Using computer technology, objects can be created three-dimensionally. So far, this technology of three-dimensional printing has grown out of rapid prototyping, which has been used with great success in the engineering industries. Sports footwear design has benefited from this computer technology. This technology allows a three-dimensional map of the body to be taken digitally and a garment then produced to perfectly fit the shape of the body.

3.21 Manel Torres
sprayed dress
The fabric for this dress has been sprayed directly onto the body to create an opaque covering.

Tina Lutz

What is your job title?
I am a consultant creative director in New York and an adjunct faculty member of RISD's (Rhode Island School of Design) apparel design department.

Please describe your job.
I work for various fashion companies in New York consulting on their design, branding and marketing strategies.

For most clients, I oversee the design team to help take the brand to the next level.

My responsibilities include everything from concept to design to final product.

As an adjunct faculty member of the apparel design department at RISD, I teach the seniors one day a week and work with them on their senior thesis collections. I hope I give them the tools they will need to realize their dreams. After 25 years in the fashion business, this is my way of giving back.

What was your career path to your current job?
I left my native Germany to study fashion design and pattern making at ESMOD (l'Ecole Supérieure des Arts et Techniques de la Mode) in Paris, France. Shortly after graduating, I joined Issey Miyake's Paris atelier where I worked on a wide range of projects including knitwear development and runway show production. After a stint at San Francisco's ESPRIT to launch a capsule collection, I returned to Miyake's Tokyo headquarters, focusing on inventive tailoring, production and design.

I relocated to New York in 1992 to join Calvin Klein as a senior designer.

In 2000, I co-founded Lutz & Patmos, a women's ready-to-wear line that focused on luxury knitwear. I served as the brand's creative and branding director for ten years.

I also focused on innovative, multi-platform collaborations and developed the notable 'Guest Designer' series – charitable partnerships with creative luminaries including Julianne Moore, Christy Turlington, Sofia Coppola and Carine Roitfeld. Joint ventures with Coach, Volkswagen, West Elm and Uniqlo dovetailed into this theme of thoughtful design collaborations.

What do you do on an average day?
Every day is different. One day I might be working in New York; the next day travelling for inspiration to remote locations; the next day I might be at a fair in Paris or Florence, and the next teaching in Providence, RI.

What are the essential qualities needed for your job?
In both of my jobs, it is important to be informed in all aspects of fashion, design and culture. It is essential to be able to translate the cultural currents into fashion and ultimately into business. You need to be flexible and able to adapt to different companies and their needs in order to create strategies that fit the client.

How creative a job do you have?
As a consultant creative director, I am happy to be concentrating on the artistic and creative side of the fashion business.

Fabric Construction

How far in advance are you working on knits?

It takes about one year to get from concept to the final garment in the stores.

Do technological advancements in knit machines affect the kind of samples you design?

Technological advancement affects all of our lives in all different areas, including knit design. I love exploring new knitting technology, but I am also a huge fan of hand knitting.

How do you put a collection of knits together?

When I put a collection of knits together, I make sure that it is balanced in different knit weights, different yarn compositions, different price points, different styles and that production is distributed evenly between factories.

Do you follow trends or do you go with your instinct?

I do not follow trends per se, but in this world where you are bombarded with information and visuals, it is hard not to get influenced by things that surround you.

What advice would you give someone wanting a job in your area of fashion?

First ask yourself what your dream job would be. Use this as your focal point and then direct all your actions towards that goal. This will help you to focus from the start of your education.

Also, for those who are looking for job security – there is a big void of talented knitwear designers in the US.

3.22

3.22 Tina Lutz
Knitted outfit designed by Tina Lutz.

The simplicity of the starting point for this project allows you to really push your design development; restricting the palette to monotone (black and white) allows you to focus on stitch work and texture. Think about how stitches can be repeated up and across the sample to create stripes, patterns and surface interest.

3.23 Knit samples
Charlotte Harris has created knit samples in response to her artwork.

You will also be designing a mini knitwear collection with your knitted samples, looking at contemporary knitwear for inspiration, but working from existing knit garments, your personal monotone research and experimental work to create your own 3D ideas.

Project A: Research and design development

Step 1: Start with your research into black and white – you could use both words or just one. Start by taking black-and-white photographs and changing the contrast to give them more brightness or tone. Take pictures of what inspires you, but also make marks, draw and take rubbings to create textures and tonal work that can be translated into knit ideas.

Step 2: Select ten photographs or pictures and with these in mind think about the kind of knit samples you might try to create. Remember, you are looking for images that suggest tones, textures, colours – not pictorial images. It will be very hard to knit a pictorial image at this stage, instead, concentrate on how you could knit textures and abstract ideas.

For example, if you are looking at a picture of a road marking, try to abstract the image; think about the width of the stripe on the background road. What are the textures/colours? What kind of stitches and yarns would best give the feel of this image?

Imagine a kitchen colander photographed in black and white, focus on the size of the holes and their repetition and how you could recreate this.

Step 3: Now select your yarns. Think of their tactile quality as well as their colour (remember there are tones of black and white). Will they be heavy or light? Hairy or smooth? The weight of the yarn must also be appropriate to the type of knitting machine you are using or the size of your knitting needles.

What proportion of black or white will be in the collection? You could just create a range of textural black samples focusing on matt/shine or hairy/smooth.

Step 4: Experiment with your yarns and stitches and produce a range of small samples.

Step 5: Select your best ideas and knit larger samples. Some samples might be two or three ideas put together to make a more complex and interesting sample. Knit six A4-sized samples.

Fabric Construction

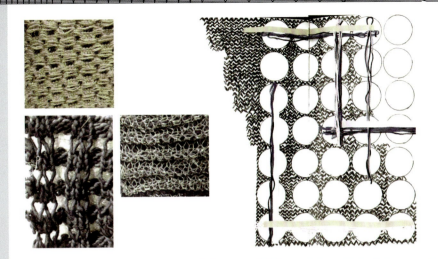

3.23

Project B: Design development

Step 1: Look at existing knitted garments that you own and make observational drawings; do not draw every stitch, but look at the basic construction and trim of the garments. Start to play around with the garments in an experimental way, maybe draping half of the garment over the stand or putting it on the wrong way up. Use your monotone research as a starting point for your experimentation. Document your 3D experimentation. Also, do some research into contemporary knitwear designers such as Sonia Rykiel, Sibling, Mark Fast, Sandra Backlund, Smedley, Xavier Brisoux, Jean Paul Gaultier, WALT and Missoni. Wherever possible look at the knitwear close up, feel the weight of the yarn and look at the techniques used.

Step 2: Now take your knit samples and put them on the stand or on your or a friend's body. Experiment with their position – put them at the collar, cuff or on the main body. Think about the scale and placement of the sample on the body – how could it be repeated and in what direction do the stitches go? Take photos or draw the samples on the stand; this should start to give you ideas for garments.

Step 3: Combine all your research and sampling and start designing a capsule menswear or womenswear knitwear collection.

Develop at least 20 fashion designs; edit and refine as you develop your ideas. Show details, fronts and backs, and look at proportions and placement, as well as finishes and trims.

You do not need to use all your knit samples, or you could combine them in an outfit or a garment.

Step 4: From these fashion designs and knit samples, produce a four-outfit mini collection. Draw your mini collection as fashion illustrations in full colour; try to show the texture and pattern of the knit.

Present your mini collection with your knit samples.

Once a fabric has been constructed, it can be enhanced or altered with the application of different kinds of surface treatments. Pattern, colour and texture can be added to fabric through techniques that include print, stitch, fabric manipulation, beading and embellishment. It is important to consider the type of technique that best suits the fabric you are working with. A loose-weave fabric would be suitable for drawn work (discussed later), whereas a tightly woven fabric with no pile is the easiest to print on.

It is wise to consider the function of the fabric, for example it could be made light reflective through the application of a print finish or quilting could be incorporated to improve heat retention. Some techniques might be interesting as a sample, but might not be applicable to a fashion garment. Consider if you are making the fabric unstable by deconstructing its structure, perhaps through *devoré* or drawn work, or if the resulting fabric becomes impractical and heavy as a result of too much embellishment. Other things to consider include whether the fabric can be successfully worn again, or whether it can be washed or dry-cleaned. It is a good idea to test a sample of the fabric you are creating by finding a dry-cleaner who is willing to trial small samples for you.

4.1 Christopher Kane
This dress has been cleverly constructed so the embroidered embellishments look like they have been stuck on with gaffer tape. A contrast between exquisite decoration and utility application.

Print can be applied to a fabric through the techniques of screen-, block, roller, mono, hand or digital printing. Pattern, colour and texture can be achieved by printing with a variety of media, including pigment, dye, flock or glitter.

Processes

Although certain processes are more applicable to specific fabrics, it is important to experiment as a fabric might react in an unexpected way. Always make notes of the processes you are trying out to refer back to later. Consider how you work with pattern on the fabric; the scale, proportion of colour, placement and repeat will all affect the overall look of the fabric and, ultimately, the garment it is to be used for.

Block printing

Block printing is one of the earliest forms of printing. A design is applied to a hard material – for example, wood, lino or rubber – via embossing or by cutting into the surface to make a negative image. This block can then be coated with ink and applied to the fabric with pressure to form an imprint. In 1834, Louis Jerome Perrot invented the mechanization of woodblock printing, allowing multicoloured designs to be printed. The Perrotine printing process enabled the mass production of printed cloth.

Hand painting

Hand painting is done directly onto the fabric using one of a number of tools, such as brushes and sponges. Hand painting gives a 'handmade' feel to a piece of fabric, but can be a slow process for producing a long length of fabric.

4.2 Xenia Laffely
The print and colour has been cleverly manipulated within this collection.

4.3 Printing blocks
Carved wooden printing blocks.

4.4 Plastisol print
Jean-Pierre Braganza designed
this wool felt cape which has a
plastisol print.

4.5 Screen print
Sample showing a multicoloured
printed fabric.

Roller printing

The flat copperplate-printing process was
introduced in the 1770s, making the printing
of large repeats with fine engraved details
possible. They were mainly one colour with
extra colours introduced through hand-
block printing or hand colouring. This was
developed into the roller-printing machine
and was patented by Bell in 1783. This
meant fabric could be printed in a continuous
length and mass produced. Printing
multicolours through this process was
developed shortly after.

Screen-printing

Screen-printing requires a design, ink,
squeegee and a 'silk screen' – that is, a piece
of silk stretched evenly across a frame. The
first step is to make a stencil of the design,
which is applied to the screen, blocking the
silk so the ink can only pass through the
'positive' areas of the design. The screen is
placed on the fabric and the ink is pulled
through the screen evenly with the squeegee,
leaving a printed image on the fabric. The
print is then fixed onto the fabric with heat so
that it will not wash off. Multicoloured designs
are created through the use of different
screens for different colours. The silk-screen
process was used as far back as the
seventeenth century. Nowadays, the silk
screen is made from a tougher nylon or
polyester mesh and the stencil is processed
using photographic emulsion.

4.4

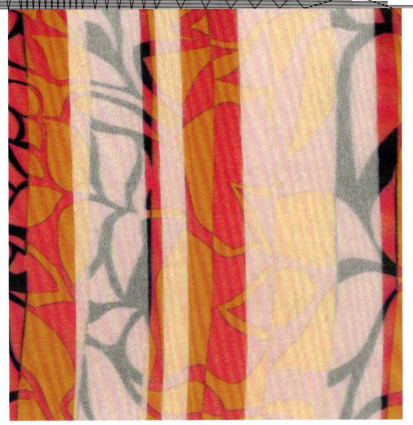

4.5

Rotary

Rotary screen-printing involves a series of revolving screens made of fine metal mesh, each with a squeegee inside that forces the print paste through the mesh onto the fabric. The design is either laser etched from a computer onto the metal mesh or exposed in a photographic process. The rotary process is much quicker and more efficient than flat screen-printing.

Transfer printing

A design is printed with disperse dyes either by hand or digitally onto a transfer paper that is then left to dry. The paper is subsequently placed on the fabric, dye side down, and heat and pressure are applied so that the design is transferred onto the fabric. The transfer paper cannot be reused as all the dye has been transferred. The sublimation process of transfer printing ensures the dye penetrates the fabric rather than sitting on top of it. This gives the cloth a good handle and also does not affect the fabric's ability to breathe. This method is used on synthetic fabrics. However, non-synthetic fabrics can also be used, but they must first be prepared with a coating

Digital printing

Inkjet printing for textiles is very different from the other types of printing already discussed because of the non-contact mechanics of the print head, but also the means by which the individual colours of a design are produced. Ink is directed through nozzles as a controlled series of drops onto the surface of a fabric, printing line by line. Usually, a set of inks is used consisting of at least three or four primary colours, namely cyan (turquoise), magenta, yellow and optionally black, the so-called CMYK inks.

As most inkjet printers were originally designed for paper printing, technical specifications are more related to those used in the reprographics industry than to those that a textile printer would normally employ. Reference is usually made to inks rather than dye solutions, pigment dispersions or print pastes. Similarly, print resolution is usually defined as dots per inch (dpi) or lines per inch (lpi). The two main digital fabric printers used today are the Stork inkjet printer from the Netherlands and the Mimaki textile digital printer from Japan.

Pigments

Technological improvements are enabling manufacturers to use pigments rather than dyes when making inks for textile printing using digital technology. Pigments are intrinsically more light-fast and wash-fast than dyes, and are often less expensive. Unfortunately, pigmented inks tend to flow less well than dye-based inks, which can be a problem when delivering ink through a nozzle. Furthermore, technological advances in digital printing have led to improvements in the way that pigment-based inks adhere to the surface of the fabric. Pigment-based inks can be printed onto a broad variety of fibres and fabrics, whereas dye-based inks are restricted to specific types of fibres and fabrics.

When using dye-based inks, the fabric must first be prepared with a chemical coating. The fabric is then printed and goes through a fixation process using steam to ensure that the ink adheres to the fabric.

The fabric is then washed to remove the coating. Pigment-based inks do not need to go through this fixation process, which makes pigment-based printing more economical in terms of running costs. Unlike dye-based inks, pigmented inks do not require a solvent to dissolve the colourant. Such solvents are often based on volatile organic compounds, meaning that dye-based inks tend to be less environmentally friendly than pigmented inks. Water-based non-toxic inks are available.

Digital printing allows the textile designer to work straight from the computer to cloth with no need for paper designing. Very high-definition imaging can be achieved and many colours can be printed without the need for numerous screens. Infinite layers can be built up within a design and clever three-dimensional imagery can be achieved. The repeat can be any size for a design, and it is not restricted by screen size.

4.6 Digital print
The print in this top by Masha Reva has been engineered to flow around the body and sleeves.

4.6

It is important to choose the correct media for successful textile printing. The media must fix to the cloth correctly and have a good handle for fashion purposes. Colour and pattern are achieved through the application of inks and pigments, and texture can also be added to fabrics through certain printing methods. Chemicals can be used to produce a 'relief' effect on the surface of the fabric or to 'eat away' at it to create a deconstructed look.

4.7

4.9

Inks

To print a colour, a dye is used with an oil- or water-based thickening agent, which stops the dye from bleeding in the design. An oil-based ink is more opaque and heavy, and tends to sit on the surface of the fabric. These inks are available in a range of colours and finishes, including pearlescent, metallic and fluorescent. Water-based inks leave fabrics with a better handle as the thickening agent can be washed out after the fabric has been printed and fixed. When printing on a stretchy fabric, a stretch auxiliary is sometimes added to the ink to improve the print quality so that it does not crack when stretched.

4.7 Discharge
Clear discharge paste has bleached out parts of this denim sample to a pale blue.

4.8 *Devoré*
A *devoré* paste has been applied to the fabric by a screen print process. The printed areas have been 'burnt' out by the paste.

4.9 Foil
This is an example of digitally printed cotton with hand-applied bronze foil in parts.

Surface Treatments

Discharge printing

A fabric can also undergo 'discharge' printing. First, the fabric must be dyed with a dischargeable colour. (You can see if a dye is dischargeable by looking at the manufacturer's dye information.) The fabric is then printed with a substance that bleaches away or 'discharges' the dye. Discharge printing is useful if a pale-coloured image is required against a dark background.

Puff

When printed and heated, the ink expands on the surface of the fabric. Expantex is a brand of chemical that produces an embossed effect on fabric and has a rather rubbery texture. Three-dimensional qualities can be achieved by printing puff on the back of fabrics that are light or drape well. The puff distorts the fabric, creating three-dimensional effects on the right side of the fabric.

Flock, glitter and foil

Fabrics can also be printed with glue then heat-pressed with flock paper. The flock adheres to the glue, creating a raised 'felt' effect. Glitter and foil can be similarly applied to produce special effects.

Devoré paste

Fabrics constructed with both natural and synthetic fibres within the warp and the weft can be printed with a devoré paste. When heated, the paste burns away one of the fibres, leaving behind a pattern where the other fibre remains.

Types of printing media

Fluorescent: Colours that glow in daylight or UV light.

Glitter: Fine monochrome and polychrome glitter inks.

Holographic: Interference, high-contrast, viewing-angle dependent.

Hydrochromic: Textiles that respond to water.

Luminescent: Invisible in daylight, visible in infrared or UV light.

Opaque: Colours that are not transparent. These are good for printing on dark fabrics.

Pearlescent: Soft, viewing-angle dependent polychromatic colour effects.

Phosphorescent: After charging with light, this glows in the dark.

Piezochromic: Textiles that respond to pressure.

Polychromatic: Colour-changing effects.

Reflective: Direct reflection of visible light.

Thermochromic: Inks that change colour with temperature.

Transparent: Colours with low opacity.

Textile designs have over the years been categorized into styles. It is important to have an understanding of these styles so that you can communicate with other designers or clients. The styles also show the wide variety of prints available.

4.10

Camouflage

Camouflage was invented as a way to blend troops in combat into their surroundings. After the Vietnam War, camouflage military clothing was worn as a rebellious statement by anti-war protesters. Camouflage became more mainstream after being adopted by the youth market.

4.11

Trompe l'oeil

Trompe l'oeil is a design that looks three-dimensional.

4.12

Toile de Jouy

During the eighteenth century, the town of Jouy in France produced printed cotton fabrics, especially a fabric depicting the printing process of the factory set in an outdoor landscape that was put into repeat. The name is now associated with a design that represents a repeated landscape or pastoral scene. The design is usually printed in an engraved style in colour on a pale background (see modern version on page 12).

4.13

4.14

Other basic patterns

Ditsy: Small clustered basic motifs scattered over a background.

All-over: A design that works all over the fabric often taking up more space than the background.

Stripes: Parallel bands of colour.

Spots or polka dots: Round circles of solid colour.

Checks: Horizontal and vertical lines that cross each other at right angles.

Chintz: A late seventeenth-century fabric glazed in appearance that typically featured floral designs.

4.10 Camouflage
An example of a camouflage in a green colourway.

4.11 All-over
An example of an all-over print designed by Jenny Udale.

4.12 Stripes
In this design, parallel bands of colour are broken for an aged effect.

4.13 Spots
An example of a spot print designed by Kenzo.

4.14 Checks
An example of check discharge print designed by Furphy Simpson.

4.15 Trompe l'oeil
An example of trompe l'oeil placement designed by Lilia Yip.

4.15

4.16

Khaki

During their years of colonial rule in India, the British Army dyed their white summer tunics to a dull brownish-yellow colour for camouflage in combat. This neutral tone was called 'khaki'. The word's origin is mid-nineetenth century from the Urdu term *kaki* meaning 'dust-coloured' and from the Persian word *kak*, meaning 'dust'.

4.16 Animal print
An example of an animal print designed by Spijkers en Spijkers.

4.17 Chinoiserie
A chinoiserie print designed by Furphy Simpson.

4.18 Conversational design
An example of a vintage conversational print designed for Liberty.

4.19 Ethnic design
An example of an ethnic inspired print designed by Rory Crichton for Luella.

4.20 Folkloric design
A folkloric print designed by Furphy Simpson.

4.17

4.18

4.19

4.20

Animal prints

Animal prints are fake printed animal skins, usually emulating the skins of big cats and snakes.

Chinoiserie

Chinoiserie is a French term for European designs based on Chinese motifs, featuring pagodas, dragons, lanterns and temples.

Conversationals

Imagery featuring everyday objects or creatures in repeat and sometimes showing a narrative. Novelty prints on underwear would fall into this category. Often, the choice of objects featured can allow for easy identification of the period the fabric originates from – the objects are fashionable at the time.

Ethnic

An ethnic design has a foreign or exotic style, usually thought of as African or Indian.

Folkloric

Folkloric designs are taken from European cultures and are often representative of a peasant style.

4.21

Floral

Flower motifs are the most popular style and are reinvented each season. Leaves and grasses fall into this category, but fruits, vegetables and trees are classified as conversationals (see page 117). Bouquets are tight ties of flowers, whereas a spray is a looser, more free-flowing tie of flowers. Sprigs are small single stems of flowers.

Geometrics

Geometrics are designs which feature graphic angular motifs that are often abstract or non-representational.

4.22

Gingham

Horizontal and vertical lines of one colour of the same width that cross each other at right angles producing a small check pattern called 'gingham'.

Hawaiian

Typically features tropical birds and flowers in a bright summer colourway.

4.23

4.21 Floral design
An example of a large scale scattered floral.

4.22 Geometric design
An example of a multidirectional geometric.

4.23 Hawaiian design
This design features the bird of paradise and hibiscus flowers.

Surface Treatments

4.24

Ombré

Ombré is the gradual shading of one colour into another.

Psychedelic

Psychedelics are neon acid prints that were developed during the 1970s.

Tartan

Tartan is a pattern consisting of criss-crossed horizontal and vertical bands in multiple colours. Blended colours are created where the bands cross each other. This check pattern, known as a 'sett', repeats down the fabric. Originated in woven cloth, but now used in many other materials, tartan is particularly associated with Celtic countries, especially Scotland.

4.25

4.26

4.24 Ombré design
An example of ombré designed by Emma Wright.

4.25 Psychedelic design
A circular psychedelic style placement.

4.26 Tartan design
An example of a tartan designed by Kenzo. Black spots have been applied on top.

Embroidery can be applied before or after the construction of a garment and concentrated in specific areas or as part of an overall design. It can be used as an embellishment on the surface of the cloth to enhance the look of the fabric, or it can be used in a way that makes it integral to the function of the garment, rather than simply as a decorative addition. For example, a buttonhole can be created with interesting stitch work and the shape of a simple garment can change through the application of smocking.

Contemporary embroidery is based on traditional techniques. Hand stitching is the basis of these and once you have learnt the principles, you have the foundation for a vast array of techniques. The three basic embroidery stitches are: flat, knotted and linked.

4.27 Embroidery sample
An embroidery sample showing French knots and herringbone, chain and blanket stitches, created by Hannah Maughan.

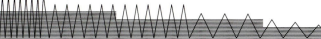
Introducing detail to fabric

If detail is required in a design, it might be helpful to first draw the design onto the fabric by hand. An embroidery transfer pencil can also be used to trace a design onto paper, the image of which can be then transferred onto the fabric using an iron.

Basic stitches

Flat stitches lie on the surface of the fabric, for example, running, satin and cross stitch, while knotted stitches, such as French and pekin, add texture to a fabric. Linked stitches are stitches that loop together, for example chain stitch. There is enormous scope for developing basic stitches. You can achieve fascinating textures and patterns by working in different threads, changing scale and spacing, working formally, working freely and combining stitches to make new ones. Also experiment with the base cloth you are working on; the key is to be as creative and innovative as possible.

Satin stitch

Satin stitch is a repeated long horizontal or diagonal stitch that sits on the surface of the fabric. The stitches are worked parallel to each other and close together to produce a flat, smooth, satiny area where the front and back of the fabric look the same. The stitch is widely used in Chinese embroidery.

Cross-stitch

Two stitches that form a cross are often used on a fabric with an even weave where the threads can be counted and the stitches can be exactly placed. Cross-stitch is often associated with a peasant look or English Victorian ladies in nineteenth century samplers.

Couching down

Couching down is where threads are laid on the fabric and small stitches are used to hold the main thread down. It is a decorative technique often used when the main stitch is too heavy to pass directly through the cloth.

French and pekin knots

The size of the knot depends on the thickness of the thread used and the number of times it is wrapped or looped around the needle to form the knot. The French knot is wrapped around, while the pekin knot is looped and neater in appearance. Bullion, coral and colonial are other examples of the knotted stitch.

Chain stitch

Chain stitch can be made with a needle or a tambour hook. The first looped stitch is held down with the next stitch to form a chain.

Blanket stitch

Blanket stitch is used to strengthen the edges of blankets or garments. Buttonhole stitch is the same, but worked with tightly packed stitches for a stronger finish.

Embroidery techniques have a rich historical background, and techniques are often passed down through generations. Many of the following styles are labour intensive to achieve by hand, but machinery has been developed for certain techniques.

Assisi style

Assisi is an Italian style of embroidery where the background of a fabric is worked and filled in with stitches, leaving the design motif unworked and in the negative. Originally, double-running stitch, Holbein and cross-stitch were used.

Blackwork

Blackwork became popular in England in the 1500s perhaps due to its popularity with Catherine of Aragon, Henry VIII's first wife. It usually features black stitches on a pale background. The stitches are flat and regular in nature, creating a graphic effect. Double-running stitch, Holbein stitch and backstitch are usually used.

4.28 Assisi style
An example of Assisi embroidery.

4.29 Blackwork
Blackwork cushion cover (twentieth century) from the Royal School of Needlework Collection.

4.30 Berlin woolwork
Berlin woolwork design for a carpet edge (nineteenth century), from the Royal School of Needlework Collection.

4.31 Crewelwork
Detail of crewelwork design for a fire screen (twentieth century), from the Royal School of Needlework.

4.32 Pulled work
'Sycamore' in pulled threadwork by Jenny Adin-Christie.

Canvas work or needlepoint

Canvas work, or needlepoint, is sometimes called 'tapestry work' as the finished stitched piece looks similar to a woven tapestry. The canvas is usually woven using a single- or double- (Penelope canvas) thread construction. Needlepoint work uses a variety of embroidery stitches, but they must be worked closely together so that the canvas is eventually covered and cannot be seen. This is best achieved on an even-weave fabric with the same number of threads in warp and weft, as threads can then be counted and the stitches placed regularly and precisely.

Bargello or Florentine work

Working on a canvas, straight vertical stitches are placed in a zigzag design and the colours of the rows of zigzag are changed to create a pattern.

Berlin style

Berlin style is a form of embroidery (originally from Germany), where brightly coloured wool in tent or cross-stitch is worked on canvas.

Crewelwork

Crewelwork is ornamental needlework, typically using crewel yarn, which is wool of special worsted yarn of two twisted strands.

Open work

Open work gives the appearance of lace, yet is worked on fabric, and holes are created through cutting and/or stitching. Examples of open work include pulled thread work, withdrawn thread work, cutwork or eyelet lace.

Drawn work

Drawn work consists of warp or weft threads that are pulled out of the cloth, and the remaining threads are held back with embroidery stitches. The spaces are decorated with stitch work and needlework, which also serves to strengthen the open structures. John Ruskin introduced the technique to linen workers in the English Lake District and Ruskin Lace has been practised since the 1880s.

Pulled work

Pulled threadwork produces a stronger fabric as no threads are taken away. The lace effect is created through stitches pulling the warp or weft away from the normal weave structure. For the best effect, the fabric is loosely woven and the stitches that hold the warp and weft back are of a fine thread so that they do not show. The intricate German derivative of the technique is known as 'Dresden work'.

4.33 Mountmellick sample
An example of mountmellick work.

4.34 Broderie anglaise
An example of broderie anglaise.
The holes create a pattern.

4.35 Appliqué
Appliqué skirt designed by
Alison Willoughby.

4.33

Needle weaving

Needle weaving is a variation of drawn thread work. Threads are drawn from the fabric and the remaining warp or weft threads are grouped and woven together.

Richelieu cutwork

Richelieu cutwork is French embroidery. Cardinal Richelieu was the principal minister for Louis XIII. He wanted France to be self-sufficient and therefore welcomed Italian lace makers to France to teach their skill. Richelieu cutwork is a development of Venetian lace. Designs feature an organic or floral pattern, with the edges of cut-away shapes defined by stitch, and within the shapes are buttonhole bars.

Mountmellick work

Mountmellick work originated in the town of Mountmellick in Ireland during the nineteenth century. A soft, matt, white cotton thread is stitched onto a closely woven white fabric in bold organic designs. Most samples are finished with a knitted fringe.

Shadow work

Stitches are worked on the reverse side of a sheer fabric, usually herringbone or double backstitch. When the fabric is turned over to the right side, shadowy shapes can be seen.

White work

The open work techniques just discussed are used in white work, but the base cloth and thread stitch are traditionally white. Typical white work also includes broderie anglaise, Richelieu, Dresden and Reticella.

4.34

Broderie anglaise

This features rhythmic and repetitive eyelet patterns, where fabric has been cut away and the edges are prevented from fraying by stitches. From 1870, it was produced on a greater scale as it could be done by machine.

Smocking

Smocking has a practical as well as decorative function, as it is used to gather in fullness in a garment. Traditionally, a garment that featured smocking was called a 'smock' and was worn by agricultural workers in the nineteenth century. The stitches and motifs used in the smocking related to the trade of the workers. Horizontal rows of dots are marked on the fabric and running tacking stitches placed at these points. These stitches are then drawn together forming vertical pleats in the fabric. The pleats are then stitched permanently together to create the smocking and the original tacking stitches are taken away. Smocking should be placed parallel to the direction of the warp and weft to avoid distorting the fabric.

Appliqué

Appliqué in textiles means to stitch one piece of fabric onto another for decorative effect. Pieces of fabric can be stitched on top of a base cloth or a reverse appliqué technique can be applied where the top fabric is cut away to form a pattern and reveal the fabric beneath. Interesting intricate designs can be created using many layers of cloth. Fabrics that do not fray are often good for appliqué work. Fabric motifs, such as badges, can be beaded or embroidered first and then appliquéd onto the garment with stitches.

4.35

Machine embroidery

Many of the embroidery stitches and techniques discussed already can be worked on domestic or industrial embroidery machines. The machines can be used creatively and flexibly to produce a wide range of effects and techniques, from controlled to more freestyle work. Domestic embroidery machines allow the user to move the fabric under the needle in order to create free-flowing designs. Most machines also have the ability to produce automated patterns at the press of a button. As with hand embroidery, the techniques can vary in accordance with the choice of thread and fabric. More complicated embroidery designs can be created on the computer and then downloaded for use on digital embroidery machines. Machines can have single or multiple heads to feed many threads simultaneously. Embroidery machines include Cornelli, Irish, tufting, loop-pile cut machines and Schiffli machines.

Patchwork

The technique of joining together pieces of fabric to make another fabric creates a patchwork; the pieces can be sewn randomly or in a geometric pattern. The choice of fabric and placement of pieces to form the pattern creates the design.

English patchwork

Paper pieces are used as templates to cut fabric shapes; the shapes are cut slightly larger than the template. This extra piece of fabric around the template is then folded over and tacked down. These fabric paper pieces are then sewn together at their edges and the tacking stitches and paper taken away.

American patchwork

Fabric pieces are cut using a template, but the template is then removed. The fabric pieces are subsequently sewn together with a small running stitch. A fabric that allows for a crisp fold works best for patchwork, for example finely woven cotton.

English quilting

Two layers of fabric are stitched together with wadding placed in between.

Quilting

Layers of fabric are stitched together to form a heavier quilted fabric. Wadding of cotton, wool, horsehair or feathers can be put between the layers to make a warmer or more decoratively raised fabric.

Italian corded quilting

Traditional Italian quilting designs are based upon pairs of parallel lines through which cord or wool is threaded to make a raised pattern.

Trapunto quilting

Like corded quilting, Trapunto is padded after the stitching is complete leaving a design that stands out in relief. Enclosed stitched shapes are slit in the back of the fabric and padded from behind, the slit is then sewn up.

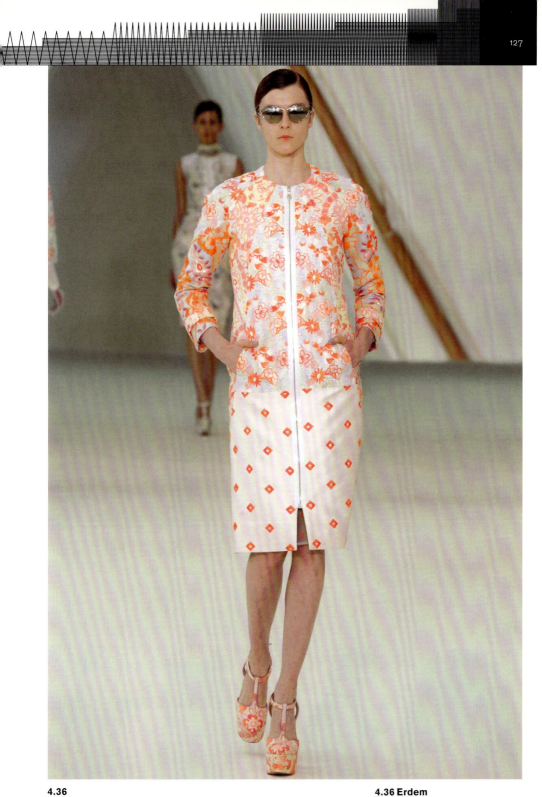

4.36

4.36 Erdem
This outfit features machine-embroidered embellishments in neon colours.

Another way to add surface interest to fabric rather than through print or embroidery is to embellish, which gives a more three-dimensional and decorative look. Beads, sequins, mirrors (shisha), seeds, shells, pebbles and feathers can be used to add colour, pattern and essentially, surface texture to a fabric or garment. Beads and sequins were used for decorative effect on the flapper dresses of the 1920s, their reflective quality enhanced by the movement of the dresses as the wearer participated in the new dance style of the time. The weight of a fabric can be changed through the addition of embellishments. Beads were used by Fortuny to weigh down the sides of his pleated 'Delphos' dresses.

4.37

In certain cultures, embellishment has been used for social identity or superstitions. Buttons, medallions and braids can show rank and power. Eagle feathers are worn by the Native Americans of North America and signify bravery. Shiny items, such as coins or mirrors, are commonly sewn onto garments to avert the evil eye.

Consider what kind of embroidery stitch and thread you use to attach the embellishment. Are you able to stitch through the embellishment, as you would with a bead or sequin, or is it held down onto a fabric with a combination of stitches like the application of a mirror disc?

4.38

4.39

Beading and sequinning

Beads can be made from glass, plastic, wood, bone and enamel, and are available in a variety of shapes and sizes. These include seed beads, bugle beads, sequins, crystals, diamanté and pearls. Beading adds texture to fabric, for example using glass beads on a garment lends the textile a wonderful, light-reflecting, luxurious quality. Beads can be stitched individually or they can be couched down, where a thread of beads is laid on top of the surface of a fabric and stitched down with small stitches between the beads. Running the thread over beeswax or a candle before threading beads helps to strengthen the stitch and minimize fraying.

French beading is the application of beads stitched with a needle and thread on the front of a fabric that has been stretched over a frame. The frame keeps the correct tension of the fabric, making beading easier and giving the work a more professional finish. Tambour beading is a technique whereby beads and sequins are applied with a hooked needle and a chain stitch from the back of the fabric. It is a more efficient way to apply beads than French beading.

Types of beads

Glass beads: Beads that are transparent, opaque, pearly, metallic, iridescent or silver lined.

Rocailles: Small glass beads.

Round rocailles: Beads that are smooth on the outside and inside.

Tosca or square rocailles: Beads that are smooth on the outside and square-cut inside to catch the light.

Charlottes: Beads that are ridged or faceted on the outside, square-cut or metal lined inside.

Bugles: Beads that are tube shaped.

Crystal and cut glass: Beads that are highly reflective with many facets.

Cutwork

Fabrics can also be enhanced through the use of hand cutwork or, more recently, with laser cutters. Precise patterns can be achieved with a laser that can also seal, or melt, the edge of man-made fabric with heat, which stops the fabric from fraying. An 'etched' effect can be achieved by varying the depth of the laser cut into the fabric and very complex detailing can be achieved.

4.37 Metal embellishment
Marios Schwab designed this neoprene and metal dress. The metal pieces can be screwed off.

4.38 Crystal decoration
Marios Schwab designed this heavily embellished Swarovski crystal dress. Each crystal is enclosed in silk net then hand stitched onto the fabric.

4.39 Cutwork
Garments by Elvira Hart have been laser cut to look like the fashion sketches.

James Stone

What is your job title?
I work for myself, but would say I am a freelance textile designer specializing in embroidery and beadwork.

Please describe your job.
I work on a portfolio of sample designs that are sold to fashion and interior companies. I work with different stitch techniques to develop traditional and on-trend designs in hand and machine. I also do commission work with worldwide companies.

What was your career path to your current job?
I studied at Norwich School of Art, UK, then The Royal College of Art, UK, gaining an MA in textile design. I graduated in 1998 and first sold work to Alexander McQueen, and this continued with more sales and commissioning from other companies in the UK. I then started a design studio called CODE and have been showing at trade shows in Paris and New York ever since.

What do you do on an average day?
On a normal day, I work from about 8 am, mainly designing new work. I travel overseas to meet clients, which involves preparation work beforehand, such as organizing travel arrangements and making appointments. I also have to chase companies to pay overdue invoices. I often work until around 8 pm and sometimes at the weekends if needed.

What are the essential qualities needed for your job?
Dedication, motivation, creativity, organization skills and patience.

4.40

How creative a job do you have?
I feel lucky to have a job that on most days allows me to do what I love and be creative. It is very rewarding to design and sell work that finally gets used within a fashion house or high street store.

How far in advance are you working on embroideries?
I often work one year in advance as clients need the work then so that they can work with the designs, and then have their mills or factories make the product in time for the store.

Are interior textiles very different to fashion textiles?
Fashion companies often use more designs as they are more trend driven and they need to get lots of products into a store quickly. Interiors can sometimes have the same design in a store for years, but they are getting more trend aware. The samples for interior companies often have to be larger as the product is larger, like a curtain.

4.40 Embroidery
by James Stone
Samples featuring a range of
techniques including machine
embroidery and appliqué work.

Do technological advancements in embroidery machines affect the kind of samples you sell?

More companies now look towards technologies, such as digital embroidery. It is a faster way of producing a design, but the traditions of hand stitch are still used – but often on a higher priced product or in a high end store.

I do find companies like the mix of the old and new, maybe an old technique used in a bold modern way on very new fabric.

How have embroidery trends changed over the last few years?

When I started, the trend was minimal, then it became more feminine and decorative, and now it is almost a mix of the two. Companies are more aware about price today, and they have to consider what they can produce on a garment or cushion, and so this affects the overall design.

How do you choose your base fabrics and threads?

I buy high-quality linens, cottons, silks, chiffons and menswear fabrics to work on and often have a good stock in the studio. I buy a colour spectrum of threads in different qualities and this can influence the style of work I do. Ultimately, I go shopping and I pick what I feel is right for the season I am designing for.

When you sell your samples, you show them in groups rather than individually – how do you choose how to put together a collection?

My work is in small collections as I think designs relate to each other. All designers are picking and choosing designs and fabrics that will ultimately work together. It normally starts as a colour idea and as a theme, such as floral, geometric, stripes and so on.

What determines the colour palette you use?

I am aware of catwalk shows and what the colours are for the next season, but I often use my instinct and use colours I like. Sometimes it is good to mix and choose colours that work together in different and unusual ways.

Do you follow trends or do you go with your instinct?

I make myself aware of the trends, but I like to do work I believe in and sometimes a good traditional look with a modern spin works well. The collection would look predictable if all of it was bang on trend.

What advice would you give someone wanting a job in your area of fashion?

I would say work hard, follow any lead you have with new and old contacts. You might have to do some work experience to get an idea of what you want to do and this is all good for your CV.

In this chapter, you have looked at printed textiles and how different styles are given names for classification, for example florals, stripes, trompe l'oeil or paisley.

In this project, you will take a classic style of textile design and through research and design you will re-evaluate, reinterpret, and modernize it to make it relevant to contemporary fashion.

In addition, you will design a capsule fashion collection for menswear or womenswear that best uses your prints. You need to be aware of contemporary fashion designers and how they use print on the body through placement, repeat and scale. Look at designers that are well known for their use of printed textiles, such as Marni, Dries Van Noten, Orla Kiely, Eley Kishimoto, Peter Pilotti, Emma Cook, Tsumori Chisato, Balenciaga, Basso and Brooke, and Holly Fulton.

4.41–4.42 Sketches
Leanne Warren is experimenting with garment ideas and placement of print on the stand in these sketches (her final designs are on page 172).

Project A: Research and design

Step 1: Familiarize yourself with printed textiles. Identify the difference between repeat prints and placement prints. Remember, repeat prints work all over a length of fabric and can be single or multi directional. A placement print is placed in a specific part of a garment, for example, around a neckline or down the front of a garment.

Start to recognize different classic styles of print design; florals, spots, stripes, etc. Look at pages 114–119 for help in identifying styles.

While researching the printed textiles try to identify different printing techniques, for example screen printing, roller printing or digital and also what medium is being used such as foil, devoré, ink, pigment and so on.

Remember to touch and feel the textiles.

Document your findings in a sketchbook either by gathering samples or photographing fabric and recording the print style and processes used.

Step 2: Using your research, choose a classic that you think would be interesting to work with. Research the style, see how it may have changed through the ages and how designers today are using it.

4.41   4.42

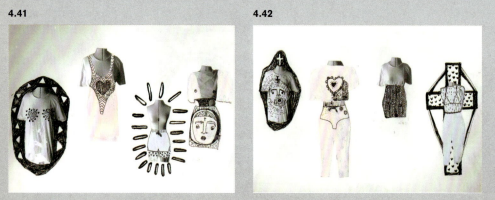

Surface Treatments

Step 3: Find some original personal research to work with. Work with something that excites you and you feel you can spend time developing. This research will direct your 2D ideas for print design and colour palette.

To develop a new style, floral for example, you could work directly from nature drawing unusual flowers from a florist. How could you do something different: could you draw them wilting or dead? Could you do a super scale collage of them and then abstract areas to create a design? Could you take objects and recreate a floral pattern with them, for example cars or wheels?

Explore traditions and conventions and be inspired to promote new design solutions.

Step 4: Produce four large drawings, paintings or collages. Think about line, tone, mark making and colour.

Step 5: Using your four drawings or artworks, develop them into three repeat prints and three placement prints.

When designing repeat prints, consider how the motifs and imagery you are using work across the page. Can you create a rhythm using the shapes within the design? Try to avoid taking one small motif and repeating it across the page, as this can create a rather boring repeat. Instead, use several motifs and vary them on the page. Consider the backgrounds to your designs.

When designing the placement prints, consider scale and position. These prints can work more like artworks as they do not have to repeat.

Project B: Garment development

Step 1: To develop garment ideas for your fashion mini collection start by taking a range of T-shirts and a stand (dressmaker's dummy). You could work with oversized T-shirts and drape them on the stand to create unusual silhouettes; you could slash into the garment and open them up, or you could combine garments together to create larger shapes. Do not force the fabric into shapes, but see how the fabric can fall and fold at perhaps the neck or sleeve.

Step 2: Draw and photograph your experimentations from the front, sides and back.

Step 3: Now you need to combine your printed textile designs with your stand work.

Firstly, print out your photographs or take your drawings of your garment stand work. Next, scan in your print designs and print out in various scales. Now, manually cut and paste them onto your stand work. This could all be done on the computer, but doing it by hand can allow you to draw and work into your designs more quickly and easily.

Think about the placement of the prints around the body and also how a repeat print works across the whole garment. Look at proportions and placement.

Step 4: Create six different garment designs using your three repeat designs and three placement designs. The garment designs and print designs should all work together as a mini collection.

Now draw up your mini collection on the figure in full colour.

It is important to understand the principles of colour and how individual colours can be worked together to create palettes that can be used within the design of textile and fashion collections. This chapter looks at the fundamentals of colour, how it is used in design and also its significance to trend prediction.

Fabrics available to a designer are influenced by trends. The colour, fibre and handle of the cloth will most probably have been designed and created based on trend information. Trend forecasters track trends and recognize new directions. Forecasters predict all aspects needed for fashion and textile design such as colour, fibre, fabric, silhouette, details and lifestyle. Forecasters do not have the ability to dictate styles. They forecast when the consumer is ready to accept a new trend and at what market level and price point. This helps designers, manufacturers and retailers select products that are on trend and that the consumer is ready to buy. By anticipating trends, forecasters enable companies to take advantage of new opportunities.

Colour and Trends

5.1 Jessie Lecomte
Styled photoshoot for a Lecomte lookbook; colour has been used to create a striking mood.

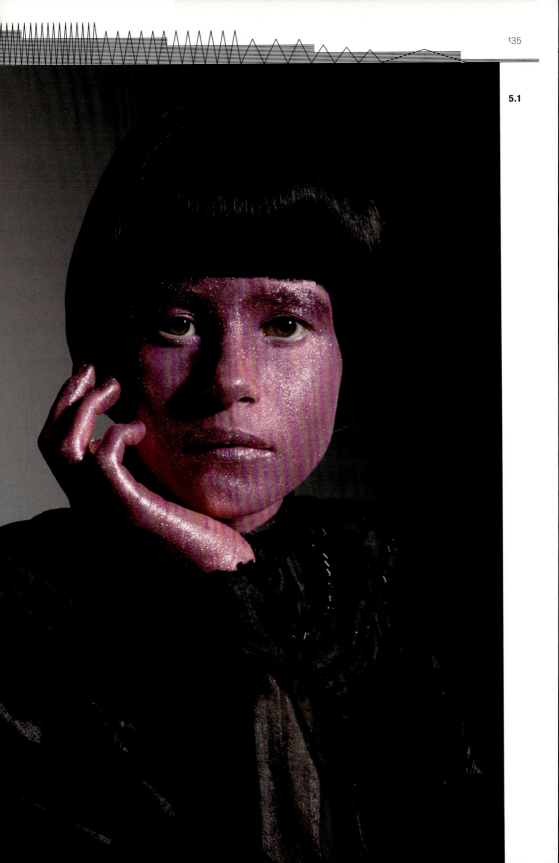

In order to successfully design a fashion and textile collection, colour must be considered. It is fundamental to the feel of a collection, and it is what the customer first sees. Colour may be chosen for a variety of reasons: it may relate to a season, the profile of a customer, the type of fabric that is available, or the concept of the designer. Colour might also be influenced by trend information and a designer may decide to produce a collection that will fit in with the colours predicted for a specific season. We first need to understand a little of the basics of colour theory and how colours scientifically work together. From this, we can start to look at how the designer uses colour within design.

Colour theory

Colour originates in light. Sunlight is colourless, but in reality it is made up of colour; this can be seen in a rainbow. Light shines on an object and certain colours are absorbed, leaving the remaining colour to be reflected back to the eye. This information is then sent to the brain, which is when we register the colour of the object. So you could simplify colour down to the colour we can touch, for example, on the surface of an object, like the red of an apple, and the colour that we cannot touch, which is made up of beams of light, for example the colour from a computer screen.

5.2

5.3

The colour wheel

Mixing other hues cannot create the primary colours red, yellow and blue. Secondary colours come from mixing the primary colours together. Blue and yellow become green, red and yellow become orange, and red and blue become violet. Tertiary colours are the colours that come from mixing secondary colours together.

CMYK colour system

CMYK is used in the printing industry. Cyan, magenta, yellow and black are the primary colours that make all the others. If you mix all four colours together, you produce black.

Additive colour system

The basic principle of additive mixing shows that when the primary colours of light – red, green and blue – are mixed in equal amounts they make white.

Red and green light produces yellow, blue and green light produces cyan, and red and blue light produces magenta.

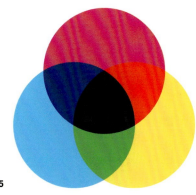

5.4

Subtractive colour system

Subtractive mixing is a principle where the primary colours of magenta, cyan and yellow can be mixed to produce all other colours. All colours mixed together would produce black rather than white, as in the additive system.

5.5

AXIS MATERIALS DETAILS

5.6

Colour definitions

Hue: This is colour.

Saturation: The purity of the hue, its richness, strength and intensity. Bright colours are very saturated. Saturation is also known as 'chroma'.

Tone: The lightness or darkness of a hue; it is also often referred to as the value of the colour. Dirty colours have more black added to them, pastel colours more white. The tone or saturation of a hue gives a colour many variations.

Fluorescent: Colours that react to light and seem to glow.

Highlight colour: A small proportion of colour used in contrast to a group of colours to lift a palette.

Tonal colours: Colours of the same hue, but range between light and dark colours.

Monochrome: A one-hue palette.

Colour harmonies: Hues that sit well together and have a good balance with each other.

Naturals: Colours derived from the landscape, sky and water.

Pastels: Colours lightened with white.

Contrasting colours: Are from opposite sides of the colour wheel and fight against each other. The contrasting colour to red is green, yellow is violet, and blue is orange. The colours that seem to most contrast one another are the primaries as they are the purest colours. The perception of colour is heightened by the use of contrasts and harmonies within a palette. A red, which is seen as a warm colour, can seem even warmer if it is put with a palette of cool colours. A pure saturated yellow can seem very bright if put with a palette of pale yellows.

Colour palette: A group of colours.

The language of colour

It is important to understand the language of colour within design. The human eye can see around 350,000 colours, but cannot remember or recall them all. It is therefore important to have a way to identify and communicate colours. Words are used to describe and give reference to a type of colour by association, for example pillar-box red or blood red. Words are also used to describe specific colour tones, for example cool colours have a blue undertone, while warm colours have an orange or red undertone. A washed-out colour could be said to have little hue or to be weak. Pastel colours have white added to them, making them pale, but not weak.

We give colours subjective and symbolic meanings. We apply our own individual characteristics and associations to colour, and various cultures see colour differently. In Europe, the colour blue is associated with a boy and pink with a girl; white for a wedding and black for mourning. In India, red is associated with fertility and is also used as a wedding colour, while white is linked to mourning. In most Asian cultures, yellow is the imperial colour and has many of the same cultural associations as purple does in the West. In China, red is symbolic of prosperity, luck and celebration, while white is symbolic of mourning and death.

It used to be that colours were common to a geographical location due to the dyestuffs that came from the minerals and plants found in that region.

Colour psychology

There is a psychology to colour with scientific evidence to show that certain colours affect our mood. There are colours that make us feel depressed and others that raise our spirits; some colours make us feel warm and others cool. Blue is considered to be a calming hue, while black and grey are seen to be depressing. These theories of colour are interesting to consider, but within fashion the choice of colour used within a collection tends to be related to artistic choice rather than psychology. Certain colours are in fashion one season and out the next season regardless of whether they make us feel better or not.

5.6 Colour palettes
Inspirational mood images are
reflected in a natural colour palette.
Copyright Global Color
Research Ltd.

The choice of colour within design is quite a personal thing. We all have our own personal palettes that we like to work with – colours that we feel are exciting, comfortable, classy or fun. As a designer, you may have to work outside your own range of colours with palettes you are not very comfortable with. It is therefore important to try and understand how colours work together, and experiment.

Certain designers are known for their use of colour. The Japanese designers Comme des Garçons and Yohji Yamamoto tend to use dark colours. Their collections are timeless and concentrate more on the clever cutting of a garment than a fanciful colour. Versace, however, relishes colourful collections to seduce its customer. Marni and Dries Van Noten use colour beautifully, their palettes are sophisticated and unusual. Calvin Klein is known for its muted neutral tones and Tommy Hilfiger for bold primary colours (however, seasonal colour trends do effect the designers colour palettes).

Certain colours, such as red, navy, black, white and ivory, are so basic they are timeless. Menswear colours tend to use these safer colours in mass-market and high-end fashion.

Texture

Of course, within fashion, a colour does not work on its own. The designer will see the colour in relation to a surface or textile, and in the context of a silhouette or garment, and this can change the perception of the colour. For example, the quality of a colour can change in relation to certain fabrics – red can look cheap and playful in a plastic, but it can look luxurious and rich in a fine silk. A black polyester can look cheap, while black wool can look very expensive (obviously this also depends on the quality of the fabric of choice). Lighter colours show texture better than darker colours. A digital print will look much brighter on a shiny fabric like silk as it will reflect the colours better than on a matt cotton.

Colour and Trends

5.7

Proportion

It is important also to consider the proportion of colour within an outfit. Sometimes, difficult or unusual colours are best dealt with in smaller proportions, but it all depends on the customer and trends in colour at the time. A new fashion colour (one that has not been in fashion for a while) may be first introduced in small amounts within a print or multicolour knit, or used as an accent (highlight) within a group of colours.

The placement of a colour on the body can make certain areas look bigger or smaller. Black is seen to recede to the eye so making an object seem smaller; this principle can be used to flatter the body shape.

Context

It is also important to consider the context in which colour is used and what it is trying to communicate. For example, in the West, a red wedding dress conveys a very different statement to a traditional white dress. Also consider how colour has been used historically for certain garments, for example, indigo denim jeans, the white shirt and the little black dress. If the colour of these staple garments is changed, do they then become faddy and not classic?

Colour can help to keep product lines new and fresh. Often, a garment does not change each season in silhouette or detail, but it does change in colour.

5.7 Bernhard Wilhelm red coat
This image shows how colour can be used in blocks for impact. Colour can be used in contrasting textures.

5.8   5.9

Season

Colours can also be seasonal. Cold seasons tend to warrant darker colours, such as blacks, browns and sludgy colours. As the season warms up, the colours become lighter and paler. They then become stronger and brighter as the sun becomes more intense. The sun bleaches out pale colours, so if you are designing for hot countries consider a brighter colour palette. Think of the colour palettes of African textiles or Hawaiian shirts. When we pack for our summer holidays, we quite often take brighter clothes than we would wear in a colder climate.

5.8 Chloé
An asymmetric top featuring a painterly print design.

5.9 Colour palette
A colour palette created by Justine Fox in response to the Chloé collection.

5.10 Pantone colour book
Colours are presented with Pantone codes for standard referencing.

Colour and Trends

Colour referencing

Colour often needs to be consistent across various fibres or fabric types, which in turn may require different types of dye that may even be produced in different countries. For a colour of a textile to remain consistent from the design stage through to development and to final realization, companies often use a colour referencing system. Pantone and the Munsell colour systems are common references for colour matching, as each colour has a specific number for reference. Rather than trying to describe the colour, the number can be used to identify the hue. Pantone charts are arranged chromatically by colour family and contain over 2000 colours. They are a great resource, but can be expensive and the paper charts need to be replaced regularly as the colours start to fade, making referencing inaccurate. The charts are also available online and as apps.

Looking at colour under different lighting conditions can affect the hue – an incandescent light places a yellow cast on the hue, while a halogen light creates a blue cast.

Colour and the customer

Colour is very important within fashion and textile design. When a customer enters a store, they tend to be drawn to the colour of a garment. They may then go and touch the garment and lastly, they will try it on to see if the fit is right.

Within a fashion collection, safe colours are usually black, navy, white, stone and khaki. Buyers will often buy in garments in these colours as they are the staple colours of most people's wardrobes. It is sometimes a good idea to offer some of the basic colours and add seasonal experimental colours to them. These colours will add life to the collection and will ideally entice the customer to buy each season's new colours, along with the trans-seasonal basics.

Skin tone can also have an effect on the colour choice of a garment. Dark skin looks great against strong, bright colours, while softer colours work better against paler skin.

5.10

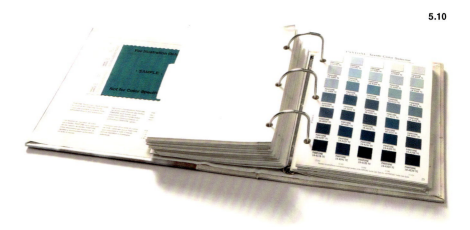

The trend industry is split into trend reporting and trend forecasting. With so much free information now available online in terms of blogging, scouting and reporting, trend reporting can be seen by anyone at anytime. Some companies like WGSN may report and also forecast.

Trend prediction focuses on a specific area of a market and tries to predict what is going to happen to that market sector in the future. It could be that the trend company is predicting what will happen next season, or what may happen in years to come. These companies sell the information they gather to other companies who do not have the time or the resources to do their own research and prediction. More often, this information is sold to companies that do some form of trend prediction in-house already. They then align their trends to those of the prediction company in order to feel comfortable that what they are designing is on trend, that the market is ready for the designs, and that it understands them and ultimately wants to buy them.

Trend companies such as Global Color Research look at the progression of trends. They monitor what has been successful for a while and evaluate whether this trend will continue and grow stronger, or whether it is time to react against it and do something different. Trend companies look at a variety of sources to inform them. They may look at what is happening in society, the economy, the arts, fashion, science, street culture and haute couture, for example. It is easier to identify a trend once it has happened; looking back, historically important trends can be recognized through changes in fashion. Trends are far clearer in retrospect.

Certain design companies are keen not to follow trends and instead be seen to be setting the trends. These companies work with their own prediction ideas and in a way operate like fine artists, developing their own personal ideas and concepts. These designers have to find their own niche market that is not influenced by trends, which can be difficult. The basis of trend prediction is intuition, what feels right and what feels new.

Colour and Trends

5.11 Trend ideas
Inspirational images, colour referencing and suggestions for colour groupings and proportions. Copyright Global Color Research Ltd.

GONE BUST:
The serenity of classical forms

25

POWDER PUFF

OMBRE

LIGHT TONES

MENTHE FRAICHE

PRALINE

CHERUB

MID TONES

KOHL

BITTEN LIP

MOUSSE

DARK TONES

5.11

Trend sources

Trend companies see that there are long-term trends and short-term trends. Long-term trends look at social trends, demographics, global trends, new technologies and processes. For example, an increase in the use of the Internet facilitates easier communication and enables employees to work more from home, so this might have an influence on fashion becoming more casual and comfortable. Short-term trends are more affected by passing fads, for example an important retrospective exhibition or a hot new designer's current collection.

5.12

Culture

Until recently, fashion was for the wealthy upper classes and nobility. The lower classes looked at what they were wearing and emulated it (known as the 'trickle-down theory'). This, however, changed in the twentieth century as street fashion started to trickle up and be adopted and reinterpreted by the couturiers. Now, fashion trends are seen to trickle up and down, influencing consumers up and down the scale. This in turn drives new trends. As street fashions become too mainstream and popular, they are seen as unfashionable by the style setters. As a result, new styles emerge.

New technologies

New technologies and processes lead to new developments within the fashion industry. These can be in the form of new fibres, yarns, printing processes, dyes or manufacturing processes, which in turn trigger new colours or fashion silhouettes, creating new trends. The copper roller-print process allowed for lengths of printed fabric to be produced first in one colour then in multiple colours. These printed fabrics can be seen in the fashions of the late eighteenth and early nineteenth centuries. More recently, the development of the circular knitting machine has allowed for seamless underwear and also Issey Miyake's A-POC concept. New developments in nanofibres are creating exciting possibilities for interactive textiles.

**5.12–5.13 Première Vision
trade fair**
A fabric fair held biannually in Paris.

5.13

Trade fairs and the catwalk

Communication is now so quick that trends are disseminated around the world in seconds via the Internet. A catwalk show in New York can be seen an hour later in London and used as inspiration for a high street fashion company immediately. Companies are able to react to this information directly and produce collections to go in-store within weeks. Trends now travel and are picked up faster than ever, therefore new trends are replaced far quicker than before.

Fabric fairs such as Première Vision and Expofil (France) and Pitti Filati (Italy) all feature trend areas. Here, a presentation is shown that highlights the predicted textures, yarns and colours for the season ahead. It includes fabrics from the companies exhibiting and colour palettes that can be purchased with colour referencing for exact colour matching.

Intuition

Within trend prediction nothing is fact; all information is up for interpretation and reinterpretation. However, it is clear that certain individuals just have a knack for interpreting information and successfully predicting trends. Natural intuition has a great role to play in trend prediction.

Shop reports

Shop reports analyse what is happening in-store at a particular time, in other words what the shops are buying and putting in-store and what customers are buying. Looking at the best stores in a city can give a good overview of the strong fashion trends for the season. It is often a good way to see the collections from up-and-coming designers in high-end boutiques. These designers may have new innovative ideas, but cannot yet afford to show their collection on the catwalk and receive press coverage from their shows.

There are levels of trend prediction within fashion. The first level looks at trends in colour. Colour groups meet from around the world to put forward their ideas for future colour palettes. These predictions can sometimes occur two years before the collections are seen in-store.

Colour trends

It is important that the chemical companies that produce dyes know what the colour trends are going to be so that they can supply appropriate dyes to the fibre, cloth and garment dye industries. It can take dye manufacturers four to nine months to manufacture dyes and send them to the dye houses. The darkness or lightness of a colour on trend will affect the amount of dyestuff that is needed; also, the kinds of fabrics that are going to be dyed affect the type of dye required.

In the 1950s, ICI produced new, cheap, bright dyes called 'Procions' for cellulose fibres, which were seen in the brightly coloured fashion of the 1960s.

The second level is texture and fabrication, determining the fabrics that are going to be important. Fibre companies, mills and weavers will look to this type of trend prediction to see what new fibres have been invented or improved upon. They look at different mixes of fibre types and how they perform, and also at the prediction for yarn weights and finishes. Large fabric companies, such as DuPont, suggest colour and tactile qualities.

The third level is surface interest, in other words, the print and embellishment for the season, for example strong print ideas and key motifs and colours.

The fourth and final level is the garment trend prediction, in other words, the key garments for the season and their details and silhouette.

5.14

Cool hunters

Cool hunters are employed around the world to find what is new and 'cool'. They usually look at underground events and movements that are not known about in the wider community, but are strong ideas within a core niche of society. They look for things such as a new band, a new store, a new toy or a new way of wearing trainers or jeans.

Colour groups

Most countries have groups that brainstorm colour trends for the home market and for export. For example, in the US there is the Color Association and in Great Britain there is the British Textile Colour Group. Colour groups are made up of the leading fashion colourists from fibre companies, fashion services, retailers and textile firms, who develop and produce colour palettes for fashion and furnishings. The palette can include a large number of colours and it is important to look at the hue, value and intensity in relation to their usage on a product range.

5.14 Marni boutique in Bejing
Cool hunters will visit new shops, restaurants and exhibitions in major capital cities for inspiration.

5.15

Packages and presentations

Packages are produced by the trend companies to sell to the fashion industry, which contain information on the specific trend areas. They may contain colour palettes with reference to Pantone colours; images are grouped to form moods for the different stories or ideas, and fabric swatches and yarns may also be included. Sometimes, the fabric swatches can be very experimental, developed specifically by designers working on the new trends.

Images of catwalk shots or fashion illustrations help to describe future garment trends. The trend packages can be quite specifically targeted to a design team's needs and not shown to any other designers or they can be more general, targeting more companies. Obviously, the more selective the package, the more expensive it will be. Some trend companies are involved in presentations where a member of their team talks through a series of images that are often presented with key words to stimulate the imagination. Some of the main trend companies are Trend Union (Europe), Nelly Rodi and Peclers (France), BrainReserve (US) and Stijlinstituut (The Netherlands). They are most successful at being able to read the clues indicating trends that are already out there or up-and-coming.

5.15 Trend package
Pages compiled by Woven Studio
that forecast colour and yarn.

5.16 Internet trend access
A page taken from the online trend
site trendstop.com.

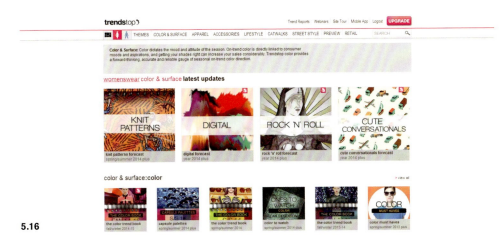

5.16

Publications and the Internet

There are various trend magazines available that include exciting inspirational ideas. These magazines commission images that sum up a trend idea. They may also commission fashion illustrations to depict key fashion silhouettes and details. Colour palettes are also featured, and there may be a round-up of the season's catwalk pictures. Some publications are very inspiring and allow the reader to really interpret the ideas suggested, others are more commercial and defined in the ideas they publish.

The Internet is a great place to find trend information through websites, such as Tumblr, Twitter and blogs, as they can be updated so quickly. Millions of other people can also get the same information, which means a trend can spread quickly. However, the downside is that a trend may, as a result, suffer from overexposure.

Many trend websites are subscription-only and as a result, information remains exclusive to the subscribers. Worth Global Style Network (WGSN) and Stylesight have offices in the major capitals of the world and are seen as the global online trend leaders. The key fashion and textile companies subscribe to their service and are given global news, reviews and inspiration. WGSN offers a free subscription to students; however, the information they receive is a couple of weeks old.

Trend prediction is a useful tool, but should be used creatively and interpreted with independent thought.

Philippa Wagner

What is your job title?

I am a future caster – I am a consultant for various clients and my job title evolves according to the role required by each and every client.

Please describe your job.

I define macro trends that will impact design decisions for business within a short- to mid-term timeframe. Looking to evolutions in technology, politics, culture and lifestyle, and aesthetics, I create a usable narrative for companies to design from. For some, this also involves working on colour palettes and materials trends that will also impact their design.

I work both on a seasonal (fashion) basis and a non-seasonal (non-fashion) basis, but always underpin my future casting with tangible 'whys', such as those artists or designers who are making waves in their fields or the way that a technology, for example, is shaping our interactions with daily life.

I research a lot and read lots of magazines, blogs and books, as well as visit international shows, such as Milan Design week and Dutch Design week to see what is happening from a grass roots perspective.

What was the career path to your current job?

I have had a varied path as my background was textile design where I specialized in woven textiles. While studying for my MA at the Royal College of Art, UK, I was lucky enough to be employed by Philips Design as part of a think tank team of agitators who were tasked to look at the future of fashion, textiles and technology. We worked on far-reaching projects that explored the future of woven digital displays, and clothes that sensed your heartbeat, and shoulder pads that acted as antennas for your phone.

During this time I realized that I had a sense of what, how and why and realized that I was what is now known as a 'trend forecaster'. At the time, trend forecasting was not a subject taught in colleges and was not the business that we know it as today.

From Philips, I moved to WGSN – the first online trend forecasting platform who changed the face of trend forecasting as we know it today. At WGSN, I was tasked to run the materials and innovation sections, as well as being a key player in their 'think tank' seasonal trends. I worked for WGSN for four years and then I moved to Stylesight, similarly an online trend platform.

Alongside this I have a partnership with a packaging designer business called Future Filter that is aimed at those businesses outside of the fashion realm who still need trend analysis to help their brands survive in this over-saturated market.

5.17

How far in advance are you working on trends?

I work anywhere from 18 months to 10 years in advance depending on what the client is looking for. For my fashion clients and for Stylesight I work 18–24 months ahead.

What advice would you give someone wanting a job in your area of design?

Be curious and be instinctual. Also, understand design. I see a growing number of courses offering trend forecasting as a skill. I don't believe it is a skill you can learn if you don't understand design first. It does not have to be fashion design – it can be any design discipline, but you have to be able to understand how something needs to be put together from an aesthetic point of view. I don't think you can be taught to be a trend forecaster – I believe it is a design skill that evolves into being able to see something that someone else has sown, and being able to water it and let it grow into something bigger.

I would also say you constantly need to be out and about with a camera, taking pictures of things that inspire you; have an antenna that is always hunting and gathering as well, and develop the ability to edit.

5.17 Philippa Wagner
Philippa Wagner at work in her studio.

From this chapter, you can see that trends are important within fashion and textiles design. Some designers set trends and others follow, depending on how innovative they, or the companies they work for, are. A trend can reflect society or it can be a very personal take on an idea or concept. Trend prediction is used, among other things, for garment type, garment shape, styling, fabrication and colour.

When trend consultants put together a colour palette, they often work with an image that contains their colours. The image could come before or after the palette has been constructed. In the following projects, you first create an image, and then from this image you create a palette. It is often easiest to put together a colour palette from an image that you have seen and the colours of which you already like. That way you know you like the colours together and enjoy their balance.

Project A: Producing trend inspiration

Step 1: Take a camera and spend a day looking around; go and visit a gallery, a garden or a grand house. Go somewhere you have never been before or go somewhere familiar, but look at it with new eyes. Perhaps look from above or look from below. Find new objects on your travels.

Take photos to inspire you and record what you are seeing; photograph places and especially interesting people and what they are wearing.

Step 2: When you return, gather objects that you found while you were exploring, or find new objects that reflect what you have seen. You could bring home natural objects, such as leaves, flowers or dirt, if you have been out in the countryside. If you went somewhere industrial, you might find light bulbs and shiny objects when you return to reflect the environment you have been in. Whatever you gather, be inspired by these things, love them for their texture and form, but mainly for their colour.

Step 3: Now, set up your objects, think about how you can place them together or apart, and whether you line them up in a study or make the objects interact together.

What is the background you are using? To create a really white scientific look, they could be placed in a white bath tub or sink. You could place them on a shiny mirror for interesting effect or maybe on a texture. The colour of the background will affect the overall look of your photographs.

How will you light your objects? Natural light will keep the colour of your objects as real as possible. You could put a bright lamp on the objects to change their colour or 'bleach' them out.

Set up the object in four different ways.

Step 4: Think about how you will shoot your items. If you can get a close-up lens, you could abstract the objects. This could also be done afterwards, digitally, on the computer.

5.18

5.19

5.20

Project B: Selecting a colour palette

Step 1: On the computer, download your photographs or scan them in.

Next, select four of your photographs, one from each set-up, and select colour from them. Your palette will include eight colours: six main colours and two highlights (see page 145 image 5.11 for palette proportion). The main colours would be used for whole garments and the highlights for trims on the garments or accessories, such as belts or bags within a collection.

The colour can be created in various ways, for example: by using the pipette tool in Photoshop to select a colour from the photos; by using colour chips from paper or magazine images (using flat colour areas); by mixing paint or by using fragments of fabric or yarn. When using fabric and yarn, you can also suggest the texture of the colour, so it could be hairy, matt or shiny.

Step 2: On a page with a clean white background set one image and the eight colour chips. Do this for all four trend colour image predictions and give each page a word that best describes the mood you have created.

Step 3: When you are next designing a fashion collection, use one of your palettes. It will give you a very original colour palette to work from. The original trend research that you undertook, photographs of places and people, can also be used to give ideas for textures, garment silhouettes and details.

5.18–5.20 Surface design
Objects have been gathered and manipulated. They can now be used to inspire a colour palette and textures for a collection.

6

This chapter focuses specifically on how textiles are used within fashion. It investigates the decisions a designer has to make when choosing a fabric, choices to do with functionality, aesthetics and cost. It also looks at how a designer can best design with fabric, working in three dimensions by draping on the stand or through computer draping. When the textiles have been designed and made, it is important to understand how to then make them into garments: and what are the best ways of cutting and constructing specific fabrics?

Textiles Used in Fashion Design

6.1 Rad Hourani
Various fabrications have been used to create a layered crisp tailored silhouette.

If you are a knitted textile designer you will be designing swatches of knit, but if you are a knitwear designer you will also be designing the garment the swatch is for. These two processes are very much connected, as the garment literally grows from the knitted stitch.

As a print or weave designer, the process of textile design and garment design are less integral. The fabric tends first to be designed as a length and then the garment is cut from it. However, some of the most interesting print and weave designs can come from the knitwear approach, where the garment shape develops along with the fabric sample so that they connect with each other.

As a fashion designer, it is extremely important that you understand what properties fabrics have and how best to use them on the body, functionally and aesthetically.

The best fashion designers have a strong understanding of fabrics, how best to design with them and construct garments from them. Try to integrate the design of the silhouette and details with the choice of fabric as you go along. Fabrics can stimulate garment ideas and vice versa. Certain designers will be known for their use of textiles for fashion, others for their details and silhouettes, but these designers still need to choose the right fabric for their designs. A poor design can be improved with a fabulous fabric, but a fabulous design rarely works in a dreadful fabric.

6.2

6.3

6.4

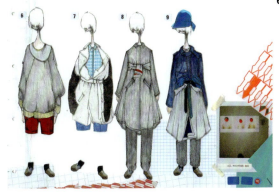

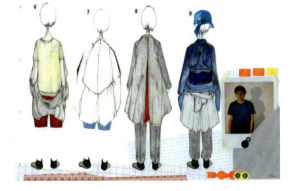

6.2–6.4 The design process
The images here show a mood/fabric board, design sketches and final line-up of garments. The use of technical menswear fabrics in strong colour is key to the collection.

Fabric choice

Consider what you are trying to achieve in your fashion designs. Are you after a flashy print or embellished garment to dazzle as a showpiece on the catwalk? Or are you designing a garment that incorporates interesting design details of cut, seam lines and darts? A woolly knit certainly would not allow for this, but a simple plain weave would work well. What kind of silhouette are you working with? A fitted silhouette close to the body can be created with a tailored woven fabric or maybe a stretch fabric or bias-cut fabric. A silhouette that sits away from the body could be created from thick boiled wool or perhaps from a crisp organza with French seams giving structure to the garment.

The season you are designing for can dictate the choice of fabric. Heavier fabrics are used more in autumn and winter and lighter, breathable fabrics in spring and summer. However, we tend now to be able to wear a variety of fabrics in all seasons as we live and work in heated and air-conditioned environments.

Consider the durability and function of the fabric: does it need to be hard-wearing or wash well for everyday use, or is it a garment that will be worn on special occasions and dry-cleaned? If the garment needs to be worn in poor weather conditions, consider the fabric and construction finishes best suited for this.

Lastly, how much does the fabric you are using cost? Is it appropriate to the level of the market you are targeting? A couture garment will feature the most high-quality original fabrics available. High street designs will be made from cheaper, high-performing fabrics that are durable and wash well.

6.5–6.7b Jan Taminiau
In this collection, designed by Jan Taminiau, each garment can be worn in two ways, so every garment came out twice on the catwalk.

The jute base cloth of this dress is tufted with silk chiffon and silk crêpe. The top layer is made of washed silk and tape-spooled lace woven with needle-spooled lace.

This one-piece woven dress is constructed from three layers of cotton, with elastic woven into it to create shape. Underneath is a boxer short.

Textiles Used in Fashion Design

6.5

6.6

6.7a

6.7b

Fabrics can be chosen for their performance and function. They could create a waterproofed garment or could be used to create an interesting silhouette through their structural properties.

Performance

As discussed in the previous chapters, performance or technical fabrics can be created at various stages of production, at fibre production, fabric construction or even when the garment is finished. Performance fabrics can be creatively used in garment design. A viscose microfibre could incorporate microcapsules containing specific chemicals that when made into a yarn and woven, produce a fabric with UV protection, which could be used for beachwear or childrenswear. Wool could be boiled and quilted to protect the body from the cold or even from pressure or abrasion, ideal for outerwear. A cotton fabric could be waterproofed with the addition of a laminate finish for sportswear.

New developments in smart fabrics can also add more futuristic properties to fabrics, for example fabrics that have a memory, can change colour or can even act as a communications interface. Designers also use technical performance fabrics for their aesthetic qualities rather than for their primary functions, for example neoprene is used for diving suits, but can also be used to create structure due to its density.

Drape

Fine fabrics that have a loose construction tend to drape better than thicker fabrics with a tighter construction. However, this is not always the case; fibre content and finishes both play a part in the 'drapability' of a fabric. It also depends on what type of draping you require; flat fluid drapes or full voluminous folds and shapes. When buying a fabric, unwind a length and hold it up to the body to see how it falls and if it is appropriate for draping.

Volume

Volume can be achieved through the use of thick or hairy fabrics, but also by using large amounts of thinner fabrics that can be gathered or pleated. Fabrics can be used in garments in such a way that they catch air when the garment is in motion, creating volume. Volume can also be created with the use of seams and darts to create shape. It is important to think where the garment is touching the body and what shapes you are trying to make between the body and garment.

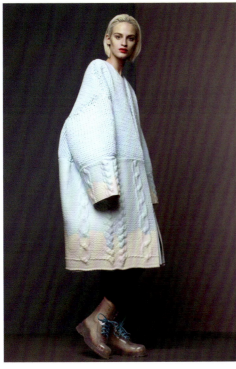

6.8

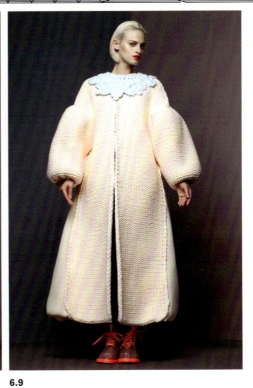

6.9

6.10

6.11

6.12

Structure

Structure can be achieved by employing tailoring techniques adopted from menswear design through the use of specific seaming methods, interfacing, canvases, padding and boning. Structure can be simply achieved by using appropriate fabrics; on the whole, a tightly or densely constructed fabric will offer greater garment structure than a loosely constructed fabric. A structured garment does not rely on the body to give it shape, you can create a shape that sits away from the body or that exaggerates the body in some way, for example a tailored suit could give the illusion of broad shoulders. Structure can also be used to control the body and force it into new shapes. Tailoring was used before the invention of stretch fabric to create new body shapes through clothing.

Stretch

Stretch fabric allows garments to fit on the body without the use of tailoring. Stretch garments are comfortable and easy to wear, allowing the body to move freely with the garment. They also support the body (powernet can be used to lift and hold the body) and if used well, stretch can be used to flatter the body. Stretch fibres are frequently added to other fibres to improve the performance of a fabric. Fabrics tend to distort when we wear them, especially in areas such as the knees, elbows and seat. A proportion of stretch in a fabric will bring the fabric back into shape after it has been worn.

6.13

6.12 Christopher Kane
In this dress fine jersey has been used to create fit and for decorative purposes it has been looped into rings.

6.13 Aina Beck
A heavy denim creates a silhouette that sits away from the body. A layer of foil has been applied to the bottom half of the garment which stiffens the fabric and adds to the shape.

Fabrics can be used purely for their aesthetics, that
is, for their visual or tactile qualities. They can be
chosen for their wonderful colour, for a beautiful
pattern or interesting texture.

6.14a

6.14b

Colour, mood and trend

The choice of textiles, imagery and colour significantly influences the message of a fashion collection. As discussed in Chapter 5, most fabrics that are produced have been designed as a result of the influence of trends. These trend ideas might then come through into a fashion collection or the fabric may be used in a completely different way. For example, a futuristic laminated fabric could be used to produce a modern, futuristic-looking fashion garment or the fabric could be used to give a modern twist to a classic piece. The use of well-chosen fabrics can unite fashion ideas into a strong collection.

Pattern

Pattern can be used to give a fashion collection a specific look, but this can have both positive and negative outcomes. For example, if a designer uses a certain pattern that is not on trend for the season, the collection may not be desirable and may not sell even if the garment shapes are good. Good use of pattern and clever placement can create a very personal fashion collection.

Pattern can be used to create a strong brand image, too: think of Pucci prints or Missoni knitwear. However, if the pattern becomes too popular it can have a negative effect on the brand.

Texture

Texture can enhance a garment through its visual and tactile qualities. It is really important how a fabric feels; fabric is worn next to the skin and is felt throughout the day. Texture can also add interest to a garment without using design details.

**6.14a–6.14b Texture
and pattern**
Jack Bebbington has combined
a variety of fabrications in this
menswear design.

You must consider where you are going to buy your fabrics if you are not creating them yourself. You may just need a length of fabric for a one-off garment or you might need to buy more of the fabric if you are going to put your fashion designs into production.

If you are creating one-off garments you could find fabric at markets, vintage fabric fairs, flea markets or on trips and holidays. If you sell quantities of your designs, you will have to think about buying fabric from a place that can supply larger amounts and that you could go back to and reorder from if necessary.

If you are buying fabric in a shop, you can see how much is on the roll and hope that it is still there if you need to come back. It is safer to buy from wholesale fabric suppliers who will have specific fabrics in stock, as they have catalogues that you can buy from and reorder. However, this can still be risky as they may not have fabric in a certain colour in stock when you need it.

Looking for fabrics at fabric fairs such as Première Vision is an option; however, for students this may simply not be realistic as fabric suppliers must sell fabrics in minimum lengths and you may not be able to meet their requirements. Also, certain fabrics that are shown at trade fairs do not go into production if the supplier does not get enough orders for them. When buying from fabric fairs, it is important to check the prices carefully and to find out whether there are hidden costs, such as delivery or supplementary (such as minimum order) fees.

6.15 Iris van Herpen
Innovative technologies have been used in this couture outfit.

Show pieces

Show pieces are garments that never get to the shop rail, but are conceived to attract press interest, which will promote the designer to a wider audience. They are intended to grab attention.

Textiles Used in Fashion Design

Consider what level you are designing for. The fashion industry can be simplified into the following categories: supermarket, high street, independent designer (producing smaller amounts of garments), mid-level brands and designers, ready-to-wear designers (that show at the fashion weeks in the main capitals of the world), luxury super brands (such as Gucci and Prada) and couture. There are also casual, denim and sportswear brands that range from small labels to the massive super brands such as Levi's and Adidas. It is interesting that most fabrics can be found at all levels of the fashion industry; what matters is the type of garment that the fabric is made into and its perceived value (that is, what the customer expects to pay for it).

However, there are some fabrics of which you will see more at certain levels; for example, sportswear and casual wear will use more technical performance fabrics with durability and stretch. Supermarkets will use cheaper fabrics, but because they will be producing huge quantities of garments they will need a lot of fabric, so can therefore buy a good fabric at a cheaper price than an independent fashion designer.

High street garments at mid prices should wash and wear reasonably well; this level of the industry is very competitive and the customer will demand that garments have these qualities. The ready-to-wear level will try to use innovative individual fabrics to set garments apart from other ready-to-wear designers. Showpieces for ready-to-wear designers may not have to perform beyond the catwalk. These textiles might never need to be washed or need to be very durable, allowing room for more experimentation. Also, the work required to create the textile may make it unfeasibly expensive to produce to order. Couture is really the only area where a fabric could be very expensive and it may not need to be washed or wear well.

Do not forget to consider whether you are designing menswear, womenswear or childrenswear. Certain fabrics might be difficult to use in menswear as they may appear too feminine. There are safety regulations about certain childrenswear fabrics too, especially nightwear. Organic fabrics are popular for babywear.

6.16 Rick Owen
The use of classic menswear fabric and colour keeps these garments wearable.

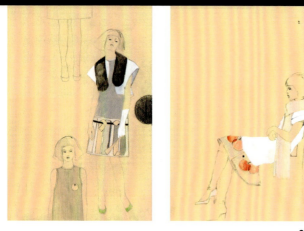

6.17

6.17 Fashion illustrations by Julia Krupp
A sketch style highlights key areas of pattern and texture interest in this fashion illustration.

6.18 Leanne Warren
Transparent and textured fabric has been illustrated here.

The best fashion collections integrate fabric design and fabric selection with garment design from the start. It is important to integrate the fabric and garment together, working from one to the other. To achieve this, select fabrics as you design garments and continue to perfect your fabric choices as your garments develop. It is important to handle (feel and drape) your fabrics when you design in order to understand their properties, for example, whether they drape and stretch or whether they are stiff and structured.

6.18

Textiles Used in Fashion Design

Draping on the stand

Certain fashion ideas are best designed in three dimensions on the stand, as working in this way allows you to see how fabrics drape or fold. If you can use the fabric you have designed to drape, this will obviously give the best results; however, you may not have yet created your fabric. If so, choose a fabric with similar characteristics in weight and construction to your designed fabric in order to get as true a representation of the fabric's qualities as possible.

When draping, design ideas are endless so consider what you are trying to achieve: what is the reason for the draping? Drape with control, do not just scrunch. Think about where the fabric touches the body and the shapes you are making. Remember that draping on the stand is not just about letting fabric fold and hang, it can also help with other areas of design such as the proportion of detail on the form, volume and placement of pattern. It is really important as a textile designer, who works in fashion, to trial your designs on the stand or body. Also hold your fabrics up and look at them in a mirror to see if colour, pattern, proportion and texture are working well.

Photograph or draw your stand work and then work into the images adding details, eliminating areas that do not work or changing proportions. Once you have created something you like on the stand, consider how the shapes and proportions you have created work with the body, how they will become garments; in other words, how you will get into them, seam them and finish them.

Working in 3D on the stand can help you understand fabric qualities. Practice drawing fabrics in order that you can translate your fashion ideas successfully with textiles.

Digital drape

There are computer packages that allow a designer digitally to drape fabrics on a three-dimensional form. By scanning in a fabric or using a virtual fabric construction, drape, colour and texture can be shown in three dimensions on the two-dimensional computer screen. The benefit of this system is that sample garments can be trialled in virtual space quicker and more cheaply than in reality. The garments do, however, look rather computer animated and designers do not really get a good understanding of a fabric unless they are handling and interacting with it.

Drawing textiles

Experiment with different media and textures when you draw garments and think about using a technique that can represent a fabric well. It is important that you can express the type of fabric a garment is made from and not make everything look like it is made of cardboard. Try to express structured, hairy, woolly, flat, smooth, transparent, shiny, hard, soft, padded, crisp, lacy, printed, embroidered and sequined textures. Explore how a fabric moves, drapes and folds on the body.

6.19

Most fabrics have a front ('right') and back ('wrong') side, the front being the side that is usually cut to be visible on the outside of the garment. Some fabrics also have a top and a bottom; they might have a repeated direction of pattern like printed, damask or brocaded fabric. A fabric may also have a pile that has a slight direction and a slight colour difference that can be seen when the fabric is draped, for example, velvet and corduroy. It is important to consider the right, wrong, top and bottom of a fabric when cutting out pattern pieces. All pattern pieces should be marked with a grain line showing a direction and they should be placed facing the same way on the fabric to avoid incorrectly cutting a piece.

Garments are normally cut with the major seams running parallel to the lengthwise grain as this helps to control the structure of the garment and there is also more stretch across a fabric. Pattern pieces for sleeves and legs where elbows and knees flex will be accommodated in the stretchy part of the fabric. The bias is at 45 degrees to the warp or weft. Garments can be cut on the bias or cross, which gives characteristic drape and elasticity to a garment.

6.19 Vintage Comme des Garçons
Seams and darts have been deconstructed in this wool coat.

6.20 Welt seam
Detail of a welt seam with top stitching, often used for denim garments.

6.21 Overlocked seam and bound neckline
Overlocking the seams of a jersey garment allows for stretch. Binding finishes the raw edge of the neck.

6.22 French seam detail
This type of seam neatly encloses and conceals raw edges.

6.23 Running seam with overlocked edges
A quick way to stop raw denim fraying at the seam.

Selvedge

This is the edge of the fabric running down the length or warp produced during manufacture so that it does not fray.

Seaming and darts

Seams and darts are needed to render a two-dimensional fabric into a three-dimensional garment (except in the case of knitwear, where darts are not as necessary). A seam can be chosen for its functional or aesthetic qualities. Garment seams need to be finished to stop the seam allowance fraying and to make the inside of the garment more attractive. Some seams can be bound or overlocked after construction, while other seams, such as French seams and welt seams, are constructed and finished at the same time.

It is important to know how best to cut seams and finish garments using the fabrics you have chosen. Good construction will make a garment far more successful and show your fabrics off well.

6.20

6.21

6.22

6.23

Seam allowance

This is the amount added to the outside of the pattern edge to allow for sewing.

Basic cutting and sewing principals

Before you make up a garment, measure a square of the fabric, then wash and remeasure it to see how much the fabric has shrunk. When lining a garment, make sure the lining fabric has the same wash qualities as the main body of the garment, as shrinkage can cause the garment to hang badly or the colour in a fabric might run.

Certain construction techniques need a fabric that can be shrunk with steam, such as a wool used in a tailored sleeve head. A synthetic fabric will not work in the same way so may not be suitable for a particular technique.

6.24

Do not let stretch fabrics hang over the table as you cut them, as the fabric will distort and affect how the pattern pieces are cut. Use stretch interfacings with stretchy fabrics if you need to retain the stretch in a garment.

6.25

Thin needles, for example size 9, are used for light fabrics including silk, chiffon and voile, while a heavier needle, for example size 18, is used for denims, canvas and overcoating. Replace needles as they become blunt for better stitching. A leather needle that has a small blade is best used for leather construction.

6.26 Toile

Toile is a French term for cloth, but is used nowadays to describe a mock-up of a garment (to check fit and make). A toile is usually made from cotton calico (in various weights) or a fabric similar to that which the actual garment will be constructed from. Toiling your designs is important as it allows you to see whether your design ideas actually work as a garment.

6.24 Internal construction
Internal construction of a La Petite S***** wool dress. It is lined with silk organza, the hem of which is baby locked and shows beneath the dress. A corseted structure holds the top of the dress, leaving the wool to hang from under the bust.

6.25 Wool dress by La Petite S***
From the outside the dress has a relaxed folded silhouette; we are unaware of the complex internal construction beneath.

6.26 Stella McCartney
Transparent fabrics with bright colour blocking panels have been layered up to create depth within this outfit.

Construction for patterned and embellished fabrics

You may need more fabric than you think for your garment if you want to place patterns and embellishments in specific areas. It is possible to engineer designs so they flow from one pattern piece to another, or think about shifting seams so that a pattern can work around the body and not be cut by a seam.

Patterned fabrics

Consider how pattern is placed on the garment. Some patterns may have a direction – a top and a bottom. How does the size of the pattern relate to the size of the garment? Large-scale patterns will need thoughtful placement; a larger garment will obviously provide more space for a larger design. If the pattern needs to be symmetrical across a garment, you must take time to carefully lay out pattern pieces on the fabric. When marking out pattern pieces for cutting, make sure you consider where the seams join and not where the edges of the seam allowance join. Also look at how a pattern travels across the body and across openings and the centre front of a garment. Consider what the garment looks like as pattern pieces go off grain; for example, a batwing sleeve placed on a vertically striped fabric will have stripes running up the body, but horizontally across the width of the sleeve. It might help to draw the pattern you are working with onto the toile to work out its position on the body and across seams.

Sequined and beaded fabrics

Sequined and beaded fabrics may need to be stabilized before they are cut so that the beads do not come off. The most professional way to work with embellished fabric is to first mark the pattern pieces on the fabric, then remove the sequins or beads from the seam allowance just past the seam line and knot off the bead or sequin threads. The fabric can then be cut without the sequins or beads falling off. Tape can be used to push the sequins or beads away from the seams before sewing and then sequins or beads can be sewn by hand over the seams on the outside of the garment. If a sequined garment is not constructed in this way, the garment might have to be lined to cover any scratchy seams that contain cut sequins or beads. Garments should be stored flat to avoid sagging caused by the weight of the embellishments.

Pleated fabrics

Natural fibres can shrink when a fabric is pleated so pre-shrink the fabric first. Flat pleats are best hemmed before pleating, whereas raised pleats can be hemmed afterwards.

6.27

Construction for knit

Knitwear can be constructed in three different ways. First, fabric can be knitted as a length, then the garment pieces cut and sewn together. Second, garment pieces are knitted to shape or fully fashioned, then sewn together to produce a garment. Finally, the garment is knitted in three dimensions with little or no seams (see Chapter 3 for more information on types of knit).

6.27 Camilla Bruerberg
Machine knitted jumpsuit featuring a tonal geometric design.

Cut and sew

Knits have different stretch qualities related to the stitch construction and fibre content, and knits can stretch across length and width, or in all directions. Consider where you require the stretch on a garment, usually where elbow and knee joints are and in the seat of a garment. Consider how much stretch is needed to get a garment over your head without a fastening.

Machine-knitted fabrics tend to twist in production so the grain is off; this can cause garments to hang badly. Follow a vertical rib or wale to determine the grain of the knit and lay your pattern pieces accordingly. Do not let the fabric hang off the end of the table as you cut it as this will cause distortions.

Silk jersey can be pinned first to tissue paper, pattern pieces can then be laid on and cut out with sharp scissors. Certain knits can ladder and will curl when cut (single jersey curls to the right side when cut). A ballpoint needle or stretch needle will glide between the yarns rather than piercing the fabric and causing laddering.

Jersey garment seams are overlocked together; this stitch allows the seams to stretch with the garment and not break. The stitch also contains the raw edges of the pattern pieces to create a neat finish. If no stretch is needed in a seam it may be advisable to stabilize it with a non-stretch tape, for example on a shoulder seam. Reinforce buttonholes with woven interfacing and hand stitch zippers in place before machine stitching them. Let the garment hang overnight before measuring and hemming, then zigzag or twin needle the hem. Knitted garments should ideally be stored flat so they do not sag.

6.28

6.29

6.30

Fully-fashioned knit

Knitted fabric that is not cut into pattern pieces must instead be fashioned or shaped into pattern pieces through increasing and decreasing stitches. Fully fashioned shaping can also create a decorative feature at the seams. Slight increases and decreases can be created by changing the stitch tension row by row, by changing the thickness of the yarn or by changing the type of stitch. A ribbed edge is a good example of this; ribbed panels can be placed at the waist or wrist to bring the garment in to fit.

In order to work out a pattern for a knitted garment you must first knit a tension swatch. Knit a 15cm square of knitting, finish it in the way the garment would be finished, for example washed or pinned out and steamed, but be careful not to overstretch the sample while you do this. When the sample is dry and relaxed, measure the number of rows (vertically) and stitches (horizontally) in a 10cm square section in the middle of the swatch. In certain swatches, you may have hidden some of the stitches in tucks or slip-stitch structures – this should be taken into consideration.

Measurements of centre-back length, cuffs and sleeve length are taken either from a person, from a garment that already exists or from a jersey toile. Now work out how many stitches need to be knitted to create the required pattern pieces for the garment shape. Trims such as collars, cuffs and waistbands will all have to be knitted also.

Once fashioned pieces have been knitted they may need to be blocked before constructing together, as they may have lost their shape while on the machine. Chunky fabrics and ribs do not need to be blocked. Blocking involves placing the knitted piece face down onto a padded stiff backing, straightening the knit and checking the measurement. The knitted piece then requires careful steaming. Do not put the iron in direct contact with the knit as this may flatten stitches. Let the piece cool down completely before removing it from the backing. Fully fashioned knitwear can be sewn together by hand using a variety of stitches including back, blanket, overlock, or zigzag stitch on a sewing machine, which allows for more stretch than a normal straight stitch. Make sure you use a roller foot or cover the foot with tape so it does not get caught in the knit stitches if using a sewing machine. There should be as much stretch at the seams as there is in the rest of the garment. Pin the pieces together first so they do not overstretch; you can use the same yarn that the garment is made in so the stitches do not show. Use a blunt thick needle when hand sewing so that the yarn in the knit stitches is not split.

Hand or electric linkers are also used for knitwear construction where the knitted pieces are pushed onto a ring of needles and a chain stitch links the fabrics together.

6.28 Vintage Junya Watanabe wool jersey T-shirt
This top features silk, cotton and polyester appliqué flowers.

6.29–6.30 Junya Watanabe two-layer cardigan
This piece clearly shows fully fashioning around the shoulders and neck.

Construction for woven fabrics

There are recognized principles to the garment construction of non-woven fabrics (see below) but with all principles rules can be broken, so experiment but always consider the finished quality of the garment you are producing.

Transparent fabrics

Transparent fabrics allow seams, facings, hems and construction to show through to the outside of a garment. Crisper transparent fabrics, such as organza, are easier to cut and sew than the softer transparents, such as chiffon and georgette. Also, the heavier the transparent is, the easier it is to construct into a garment. Difficult fabrics easily distort when cutting and sewing. To help avoid this, lay the fabric on the cutting table to rest overnight, roll it out flat on tissue paper with no overhang, then pin the fabric to the paper and carefully cut out the pattern pieces. The tissue can be left on the pieces while they are sewn together and then carefully ripped off after construction. The seams used can affect the drape and structure of the garment so try testing different types of seams first to see what works best. Very light transparent fabrics are often French seamed. As the seams can be seen from the outside, this type of construction is very desirable. The selvedge of the fabric can be successfully used as a finish of a seam.

Darts can be very hard to achieve successfully; maybe consider how seams can be placed to avoid darts. Leave garments to hang before hemming them to allow the fabric to drop; the hem can then be measured from the floor up, trimmed and sewn. Iron transparent fabrics at a lower temperature than heavier fabrics made from the same fibres.

6.31

6.32

6.31–6.32 Comme des Garçons blouse
Cotton calico lining can be seen through the transparent viscose outer layer, enabling the internal and external elements of the garment to work together.

6.33

Pile fabrics

Check the direction of piled fabrics – there might be an up and down that will create a slight tonal colour difference on pattern pieces and garments. When cutting fabric, mark the pile direction on the back of the fabric or on the selvedge edge and then lay all the pattern pieces in the same direction. Pile fabrics tend to shift when they are right side to right side, so lay fabric out wrong side together or completely flat. When pinning pattern pieces to velvet, put the pins in the seam allowance as they can mark the fabric. To avoid fabrics shifting when you are creating seams, hold fabrics taut when stitching or stitch with tissue in-between the fabric. Be careful when pressing these fabrics as it can spoil the pile, so press from the wrong side only.

Outerwear fabrics

Seams used for outerwear fabrics often need to be strong and durable; a welt seam, which features topstitching, is often chosen. Running a plastic coating along the seam from the inside can create a waterproof seam.

French seams

To create a French seam, place the wrong sides of the fabric together and sew on the seam line. Next, trim the seam allowance down, press the seam open to flatten and then press the seam allowance to one side. Put the right sides together and sew a line of stitching that traps in the seam allowance.

6.33 Lou Dalton coat
Outerwear garment construction has been used on this overcoat.

Non-woven fabrics

These fabrics do not follow the requirements for woven and knitted fabrics, for example they will not fray, so do not need a finish to prevent this. But their construction into a garment will need careful consideration.

Leather and suede

Leather and suede skins do not come as a length, but are specific to the size of the animal they come from. Think how big your pattern pieces are; you may have to create more seams in a garment if the skins are not big enough. Seams are easier to sew than darts, so try to use seams to create shape and fit rather than darts. When choosing skins check them for imperfections, thinning and holes that you might have to work around; also compare skins for colour matching and pattern. Suede may have a nap so this must be considered when choosing skins and when sewing them up.

When cutting out use weights to hold down the pattern pieces, as pins will mark the leather. Wedge-point needles or leather needles cut cleanly through leather and suede, while a normal needle tends to rip the skin as it punctures the hard surface. Needle holes cannot be removed so take care when sewing seams, especially topstitching. It may be necessary to put a leather or Teflon foot on the machine to stop the leather sticking while sewing.

When sewing leather, press out seams from the wrong side and if they do not lie flat, glue the seam allowance down and lightly hammer from the back, being careful not to mark the leather on the right side. A very heavy leather might best be sewn with an overlapped seam; this is done by removing the seam allowance from one of the sides of the seam, overlapping the other and topstitching down. It might be necessary to stick the surfaces first so they do not slip. If the leather is heavy, slash and glue darts, or topstitch or overlap to create a flat finish. Leather stretches, but does not return to its original shape so it may be necessary to tape seams that are under strain from wear and tear.

6.34 Acne pre-fall collection fur coat
Fur has been used on both sides in this coat, which has a simple oversized silhouette.

6.35 Camilla Bruerberg
This leather jacket has been digitally printed.

6.34

Fur

Fur can be bought as tails, pelts or fur plates. Fur plates are fabrics created by sewing together smaller scraps of fur. When buying fur, consider the size of your pattern pieces. Look for an overall good even coverage and colouration, pull the fur to see if it comes out, also see how soft and flexible the skin is as it may have dried out and not be worth buying. It might be possible to patch any holes and splits on the under leather side, as long as it does not affect the look on the fur side. It may also be possible to recycle dated second-hand fur garments into something new. When cutting out fur, lay right side down and place the pattern pieces in reverse on top, then cut through the leather skin and pull apart the fur or hair. Try not to trap long hairs or fur into seams, push them away from the seams before sewing. After seaming, cut away fur or hair from the seam allowance to remove bulk and give a better finish.

Plastics

Plastics should be treated in a similar way to leather as they may show needle holes, so take care when stitching. Be careful when pressing – do not melt the fabric.

6.35

Anne Sofie Madsen

What is your job title?

I am creative director of Anne Sofie Madsen.

Please describe your job.

I create a womenswear line every season that consists of ready-to-wear and made-to-measure garments.

What was your career path to your current job?

I studied at the Royal Danish Academy of Fine Arts and then trained under John Galliano in Paris. I also worked for acclaimed trend forecasters, Peclers, before moving to London to work for Alexander McQueen as junior designer.

What do you do on an average day?

My working hours are usually very long, I get to the studio really early and stay really late. I have meetings some days that last the whole day, and other times I just stay in the studio and draw or sew, start putting together the garments and helping interns. It gets even more hectic and stressful once we are closer to fashion week, then I hardly get any sleep.

What are the essential qualities needed for your job?

Be a hard worker, have perseverance and also flexibility, and you really have to love what you do because you spend many hours doing it.

How creative a job do you have?

Very creative, but of course I also do a lot of office work.

Where do you start your research for each collection? Do you follow trends, or do you go with your instinct?

I follow my interests and instincts, not trends. I start my research in various places. I go to museums, libraries and look at ancient national costume designs and techniques. I look at various photographs, fine art and watch films.

How did you learn the many craft techniques you employ?

I learnt the techniques I use from my previous work experience, but also I research any technique that interests me and will, for example, watch online videos.

How much is handcrafted and how much do you use digital technology?

Many of my designs include my hand-drawn illustrations, and if it wasn't for digital technology I would not be able to put them on my garments. However, I always try to do half handcrafted pieces and half digital.

6.36–6.37 Anne Sofie Madsen
Dresses featuring pleated panels and intricate hand embellishment.

6.36

6.37

How do you develop your garment silhouette and details?

When creating the garments for a collection, I spend a lot of time developing the techniques (which vary a lot for each collection); most is done on a mannequin. The actual making of the garments can range from two months on detailed dresses, to two days on other things. That being said, the whole collection creation process is always a work in progress; we keep trying out new techniques, compositions and mixes of materials on the garments. To me, creating a piece for a collection is not about not thinking about the garment in itself – but the expression within a shape, material or colour.

What comes first: the idea for the fabric or for the garment?

I come up with ideas for silhouettes and techniques and then I start to experiment with various fabrics and start sketching.

How many pieces are in each collection?

The amount of pieces changes each collection, but around 25 to 27 pieces.

What advice you would give someone wanting a job in your area of fashion?

Work hard and get as much experience as you can – hard work pays off.

This chapter has covered various aspects of choosing the right textiles for a fashion design and how it can give direction to the design of the garment. This project helps you to gain knowledge of 3D silhouette development and how this can translate into fashion design ideas. Work with garments on the stand to develop your 3D ideas. Taking existing garments allows you to see how clothes are constructed and finished, also how the handle of the fabric influences the design of the garment: does the fabric create drape or structure?

Choose garments with interesting textile qualities or design details, and apply the use of basic making skills to deconstruct and then reconstruct a garment.

Project A: Research

Step 1: Find a poem that inspires you. Develop your own visual narrative to this poem to influence and inspire this project; this will help you to have a direction for your ideas. Put imagery that you can find, or have created, relating to your narrative for the poem, into a sketchbook.

Step 2: Source existing garments from home or thrift shops; look for garments in unusual fabrics or with interesting details such as collars, cuffs and pockets. These can be knitted garments or woven garments. However, do consider how you would combine stretch and woven together, as their different qualities can sometime lead to difficulties in construction later on.

Step 3: Analyse the garments you have found – make some observational drawings of them, flat on the ground or on a stand. Study their construction, where the seams are, what kind of seams have been used, look at darts, pocket types, collar lengths and how these details relate, in proportion, to the rest of the garment. This helps you to understand the garment and give ideas to what you could deconstruct later.

6.38

6.38 Stand work
Annie Ovcharenko is trying out deconstruction ideas with garments on the stand.

Project B: 3D development

Step 1: Now start to work with the garments. Place or drape them on the stand or on a person. Consider the mood and narrative you have set with your poem choice. Is there any imagery that you found that could help you with your stand work?

Think what you could take apart, or how you could create a new silhouette. You could take the sleeves from a printed floral dress and then cut and appliqué the flowers from the sleeves back onto the main body in an unusual way. You could put a jacket on upside down or inside out and see what happens. Maybe take three lace collars from different blouses and layer them up to make one new collar on a new garment. You could take a variety of knitted jumpers and undo their seams and re-stitch them to create a large strange-shaped garment that you could then remodel on the stand.

Avoid fitting everything to the stand using darts; instead, think about the shapes you can create between the stand and the garment. Think about the points of contact between the garment and the stand.

Creative design thinking for this project is related to form, line, cut, fit, shape, silhouette, proportion, detail, hang, balance, texture and pattern.

Experiment for at least four hours until you decide on your final idea. Record all your experiments either by sketching or photographing.

Step 2: Once you have decided on a design, start to deconstruct and reconstruct the garment to reflect the ideas behind your poem.

Refer to the knowledge you have of garment construction and finishes. For example, if you put topstitching on something it will look more casual, like a jean finish. If you leave raw edges, it will look deconstructed and unfinished. Also consider the fabrics you are working with; if you are using a fine transparent fabric, your seams and finishes would be different to using denim. If you are using a highly decorative fabric, you may choose to keep the garment construction quite simple.

Step 3: Create your own fashion statement by styling your garment and using it in a photo shoot. Think carefully about your choice of model and location; take inspiration from your poem.

The intention of this book has been to try and cover all the areas relating to the research, design and creation of fashion textiles. The aim has been to give an insight into the topics textile designers should know about in order to really understand their subject, and to provide information that fashion designers will benefit from in order to improve their textile work. This includes fibre qualities and fabric finishes, together with practical information on how to work, cut and sew textiles into garments.

I hope that the information about careers for textile designers in the fashion industry is useful. Quite often, textile designers do not get credited for their amazing work, leaving the fashion designer to pick up all the acclaim.

Textile design is often the unsung hero of fashion design; however, without innovative textile designs, fashion design would surely not be as interesting.

Fashion can be a difficult industry in which to work, but also a very interesting and exciting one, so try to be the best you can. Use the information in this book to inform and stimulate your designs. Continue to research topics that have not been covered in detail here. It is important to really push your ideas, be innovative, experimental and, above all, take pleasure in what you are doing.

This book has been a challenge to compile, as there was so much to look at; the more I researched the more I wanted to know. I personally have learnt so much more about textiles through writing this book and learnt even more revising this second edition. I hope you get as much out of it as I have done.

6.39 Aina Beck
This coat was first screen printed with white on black knitwear, then certain sections were hand painted, the designer treated it like a canvas piece before putting the pattern pieces together.

Textiles and Fashion

6.39

Brand image: Tangible and intangible characteristics that identify a brand.

Camouflage: Fabric originally developed by the French army during the First World War to disguise soldiers during field combat. The abstract coloured patterns have now been developed and adopted in fashion.

Classic: A garment that has a widespread acceptance over a period of time and is well known by name.

Colourfastness: How a fabric's colour reacts to washing, abrasion or light.

Colourways: Colour groups and combinations offered.

Computer-aided design (CAD): The use of computers to design.

Drape: The way a fabric hangs.

Empire line: Dresses worn during the First Empire in France (1804–1815), which were characterized by a high waistline.

Engineered designs: Designs that are made to fit into a shape or are placed in a certain way.

Fashion week: Periods of time, usually twice a year, during which fashion collections are shown in the major fashion capitals of the world to press and buyers, for example, New York, London, Paris and Milan.

Felted: The knotting together of fibres through heating with chemicals or friction, to produce a matted material.

Finishes: Processes and techniques that are used to manipulate the appearance, characteristics, performance or handle of a fabric. Also used to describe the way a garment is neatened during construction, for example, with seams, hems and facings.

Fully fashioned: The shaping of a knitwear garment so that each edge is a selvedge and will not unravel.

Gauge: The number of rows and/or stitches per length/width of a knitted fabric. For example, five stitches per inch.

Handle: The tactile quality of a fabric.

Interfacing: Fabric placed between the garment and facing to add body, strength or structure.

Japonisme: The influence of Japanese arts on Western art.

Lining: Fabric used on the inside of a garment to hide the construction. It extends the garment's life as it helps to retain the shape and also makes the garment more comfortable to wear.

Mainstream: Trends that are accepted by the majority.

Moodboard: A collection of images, colours, objects or fabrics that are grouped together to express visually a theme or design idea.

Pattern pieces: The shapes that make up a garment in paper form, created through pattern cutting.

Penelope canvas: A double mesh canvas formed with pairs of crosswise and lengthwise intersecting threads.

Performance fabrics: High-tech fabrics that were originally developed for sportswear or extreme climate outerwear, but are now used for mainstream fashion.

Overlocking: Mostly used in knitwear for cut-and-sew production to cover cut edges and seams at the same time.

Smart textiles: Fabrics that respond to changes in their environment and alter in some way. Smart fabrics appear to 'think'.

Stand: A dressmaking mannequin or dummy.

Topstitch: To stitch on the right side of the garment.

Allen, J., 1989. *John Allen's Treasury of Machine Knitting Stitches.* David & Charles.

Allen, J., 1985. *The Machine Knitting Book: How to Design and Create Beautiful Garments on Your Knitting Machine.* Dorling-Kindersley.

Bendavid-Val, L., ed., 2004 *In Focus: National Geographic Greatest Portraits.* National Geographic Society.

Black, S., 2002. *Knitwear in Fashion.* Thames & Hudson.

Braddock Clarke, S.E. and O'Mahony, M., 2005. *Techno Textiles: Revolutionary Fabrics for Fashion Design.* Thames & Hudson.

Brannon, E.L., 2005. *Fashion Forecasting.* 2nd ed. Fairchild Publications.

Brittain, J., 1989. *Needlecraft: Pocket Encyclopedia.* Dorling-Kindersley.

Campbell-Harding, V. and Watts, P., 1993/2003. *Bead Embroidery.* Batsford.

Compton, R., 1983. *The Complete Book of Traditional Knitting.* Batsford.

Cumming, R., and Porter, T., 1990. *The Colour Eye.* BBC Books

Fogg, M., 2006. *Print in Fashion: Design and Development in Textile Fashion.* Batsford.

Franklin, T. A. and Jarvis, N., 2005. *Contemporary Whitework.* Batsford.

Fukai, A., 2005. *Fashion in Colors: Cooper-Hewitt National Design Museum,* Assouline.

Fukai, A., 2002. *Fashion: A History from the 18th to the 20th Century. The Collection of The Tokyo Costume Institute.* Taschen.

Gale, C. and Kaur, J., 2004. *Fashion and Textiles: An Overview.* Berg.

Gale, C. and Kaur, J., 2002/2006. *The Textiles Book.* Berg.

Gillow, J. and Sentence, B., 1999/2006. *World Textiles: A Visual Guide to Traditional Techniques.* Thames & Hudson.

Ginsburg, M., 1991. *The Illustrated History of Textiles.* Studio Editions.

Griffiths, A., 1989. *An Introduction to Embroidery.* Mallard Press.

Hencken Elsasser, V., 2005. *Textiles: Concepts and Principles.* 2nd ed. Fairchild Publications.

Holbourne, D., 1979. *The Book of Machine Knitting.* Batsford.

Jackson, L., 2001. *Robin and Lucienne Day: Pioneers of Contemporary Design.* Mitchell Beazley.

Joyce, C., 1993. *Textiles Design: The Complete Guide to Printed Textiles for Apparel and Home Furnishing.* Watson-Guptill.

Kendall, T., 2001. *The Fabric and Yarn Dyer's Handbook: Over 100 Inspirational Recipes to Dye and Pattern Fabric.* Collins & Brown.

Kraatz, A., 1989. *Lace: History and Fashion.* Thames & Hudson.

Krevitsky, N., 1966. *Stitchery: Art and Craft.* Reinhold Publishing.

Lee, S., 2005. *Fashioning the Future: Tomorrow's Wardrobe.* Thames & Hudson.

McNamara, A. and Snelling, P., 1995. *Design and Practice for Printed Textiles.* Oxford University Press.

Meller, S. and Elffers, J., 1991/2002. *Textile Design: 200 Years of Pattern for Printed Fabrics Arranged by Motif, Colour, Period and Design.* Thames & Hudson.

Phaidon Press, ed., 1998/2001. *The Fashion Book.* Phaidon Press.

Schaffer, C., 1994/1998. *Fabric Sewing Guide (Updated Edition).* Krause Publications.

Seiler-Baldinger, A., 1994. *Textiles: A Classification of Techniques.* Crawford House Press.

Sorger, R. and Udale, J., 2006. *The Fundamentals of Fashion Design.* AVA Publishing.

Tymorek, S., ed., 2001. *Clotheslines: A Collection of Poetry and Art.* Abrams.

Watt, J., 2003. *Ossie Clark: 1965–74.* V&A Publications.

Wells, K., 1997/1998. *Fabric Dyeing and Printing.* Conran Octopus.

FRANCE

Fédération Française de la Couture, du Prêt-à-Porter des Couturiers et des Créateurs de Mode

www.modeaparis.com
Under various departments, it oversees French couture and the ready-to-wear design industry for menswear and womenswear. The federation organizes the Paris fashion shows and events at Mode à Paris.

HONG KONG

Hong Kong Trade Development Council

www.hkfashionweek.fw.com
Hong Kong Fashion Week is organized by the Trade Development Council.
www.tdctrade.com

ITALY

Camera Nazionale della Moda Italiana (National Chamber for Italian Fashion)

www.cameramoda.it
An association that disciplines, co-ordinates and promotes the development of Italian fashion. It organizes the Italian Fashion Week.

JAPAN

Council of Fashion Designers, Tokyo

www.cfd.or.jp
Promotes Japanese fashion.

UK

British Fashion Council (BFC)

5 Portland Place
London W1B 1PW
Tel: +44 (0)20 7636 7788
www.londonfashionweek.co.uk
Owns and organizes London Fashion Week and the British Fashion Awards. It also helps British fashion designers.

The Department of Trade and Industry (DTI)

1 Victoria Street
London SW1H 0ET
www.dti.gov.uk
Business advice on export and legal issues.

Fashion employment agencies

www.denza.co.uk
Agency for fashion.
www.smithandpye.com
Agency for fashion.

Portobello Business Centre

www.pbc.co.uk
Runs excellent business courses for fashion designers and provides advice on finding finance.

Prince's Trust

www.princes-trust.org.uk
Advice and finance for small business start-ups.

USA

Council of Fashion Designers of America

www.cfda.com
Promotes and advises American fashion designers.

Olympus Fashion Week

www.olympusfashionweek.com
America's Fashion Week held in New York.

Publications and magazines

10

Another Magazine

Arena

Bloom

Collezioni

Dazed & Confused

Drapers Record

Elle

Elle Decoration

Homme

i-D

In Style International

Textiles

Marie Claire

Marmalade

Numéro

Oyster

Pop

Selvedge

Tank

Textile

View

View on Colour

Viewpoint

Visionaire

Vogue

W

WWD

Women's Wear Daily

Textiles and Fashion

Museums

The Bata Shoe Museum
327 Bloor Street West,
Toronto, Ontario,
Canada M5S 1W7
www.batashoemuseum.ca

Costume Gallery
Los Angeles County Museum of
Art, 5905 Wilshire Boulevard,
Los Angeles, CA 90036, US
www.lacma.org

The Costume Institute The Metropolitan Museum of Art
1000 5th Avenue at 82nd
Street, New York, NY
10028–0198, US
www.metmuseum.org

Fashion Museum
Assembly Rooms,
Bennett Street,
Bath BA1 2QH, UK
www.fashionmuseum.co.uk

Galeria del Costume
Amici di palazzo pitti
Piazza Pitti,
1 50125 Firenze, Italy
www.polomuseale.firenze.it

Kobe Fashion Museum
Rokko Island,
Kobe, Japan
www.fashionmuseum.or.jp

The Kyoto Costume Institute
103 Shichi-jo Goshonouchi,
Minamimachi Kyoto,
600–8864, Japan
www.kci.or.jp

MoMu
Antwerp Fashion ModeMuseum,
Nationalestraat 28,
2000 Antwerpen, Belgium
www.momu.be

Musée des Arts décoratifs
Musée des Arts de la mode
et du textile,
107 rue de rivoli
75001 Paris, France
www.ucad.fr

Musée de la Mode et du Costume
10 avenue Pierre 1er de serbie
75116 Paris, France

Musée des Tissus et des Arts décoratifs de Lyon
34 rue de la charité
69002 Lyon, France
www.musee-des-tissus.com

Museum at the Fashion Institute of Technology
7th Avenue at 27th Street,
New York,
NY 10001–5992, US
www.fitnyc.edu/museum

Museum of Fine Arts, Boston Avenue of the arts
465 Huntington Avenue,
Boston, Massachusetts
02115–5523, US
www.mfa.org

Museum Salvatore Ferragamo
Palazzo Spini Feroni
Via Tornabuoni 2,
Florence 50123, Italy
www.salvatoreferragamo.it

Victoria and Albert Museum (V&A)
Cromwell Road,
London SW7 2RL, UK
www.vam.ac.uk

Wien Museum
Fashion collection with public
library (view by appointment),
Hetzendorfer Straße 79,
1120 Vienna,
Austria
www.wienmuseum.at

Fabrics and trims

Broadwick Silks
9–11 Broadwick Street,
London W1F 0DB, UK
www.broadwicksilks.com

Elegant Fabrics, NYC
222 West 40th St,
New York, NY 10018, US
www.nyelegantfabrics.com

Kleins
5 Noel Street,
London W1F 8GD, UK
www.kleins.co.uk

M&J Trimming
1008 6th Ave,
New York, NY 10018, US
www.mjtrim.com

UK Cloth House
47 Berwick Street,
London W1F 8SJ, UK
www.clothhouse.com

VV Rouleaux
54 Sloane Square,
London SW1W 8AX, UK
www.vvrouleaux.com

Whaleys (Bradford) Ltd
Harris Court, Great Horton,
Bradford BD7 4EQ, UK
www.whaleys-bradford.ltd.co.uk

NY Elegant Fabric
NYC 222 West 40th St,
New York, NY 10018, US
www.nyelegantfabrics.com

M&J Trimming
1008 6th Ave,
New York, NY 10018, US
www.mjtrim.com

Websites

www.catwalking.com

www.costumes.org

www.fashion.about.com

www.fashion-era.com

www.fashionoffice.org

www.hintmag.com

www.infomat.com

www.londonfashionweek.co.uk

www.premierevision.fr

www.promostyl.com

www.style.com

www.wgsn-edu.com

Fashion forecasting

www.edelkoort.com

www.itbd.co.uk

www.londonapparel.com

www.modeinfo.com

www.peclersparis.com

www.wgsn-edu.com

Fashion trade shows

www.informat.com

www.magiconline.com

www.pittimmagine.com

www.premierevision.fr

www.purewomenswear.co.uk

Fashion designers

Acne
www.acnestudios.com

Aina Beck
www.ainabeck.com

Alexander McQueen
www.alexandermcqueen.com

Alexander Wang
www.alexanderwang.com

Anne Sofie Madsen
www.annesofiemadsen.com

Biocouture
www.biocouture.co.uk

Brooke Roberts
www.brookeroberts.net

Camilla Bruerberg
www.camillabruerberg.com

Chloé
www.chloe.com

Comme des Garçons
www.comme-des-garcons.com

CP Company
www.cpcompany.co.uk

Erdem
www.erdem.com

Givenchy
www.givenchy.com

Iris van Herpen
www.irisvanherpen.com

Issey Miyake
www.isseymiyake.com

Jean-Pierre Braganza
www.jeanpierrebraganza.com

Jenny Udale
jennnyudale@hotmail.com

Johan Ku
www.johanku.com

Julia Krupp
www.juliakrupp.com

Kenzo
www.kenzo.com

Kyuchi
www.kuyichi.com

La petite S***
www.la-petite-s.com

Lecomte
www.jessielecomte.com

Leutton Postle
www.leuttonpostle.com

Lou Dalton
www.loudalton.com

Manel Torres
www.fabricanltd.com

Marc by Marc Jacobs
www.marcjacobs.com

Marios Schwab
www.mariosschwab.com

Marloes ten Bhömer
marloestenbhomer.
squarespace.com

Marni
www.marni.com

Mary Katrantzou
www.marykatrantzou.com

Patrick Li
www.patrick-li.com

Peter Jensen
www.peterjensen.co.uk

Rick Owens
www.rickowens.eu

Sandra Backlund
www.sandrabacklund.com

Sonia Rykel
www.soniarykiel.com

Tina Lutz
www.tinalutz.com

Viktor and Rolf
www.viktor-rolf.com

Xavier Brisoux
www.xavier-brisoux.
lexception.com

I would like to warmly thank all the people (in no particular order) who have kindly contributed to this book:

Patrick Li, Kuyuchi, Nikki Gabriel, Brooke Roberts, Biocouture, A-lab Milano, Lou Dalton, Jessica Leclere, Johan Ku, Xavier Brisoux, Leutton Postle, Christian Wijnants, Rory Crichton, Nanna van Blaaderen, Eleanor Amorosa, Laura Theiss, Xenia Laffely, Masha Reva, Lilia Yip, Spijkers en Spijkers, Alison Wilhoughby, Erdem, Marni, Rad Hourani, Jan Taminiau, Aina Beck, Camilla Bruerberg, Acne, Sonia Rykiel, Woven, Sandra Backlund, Peter Jensen, Marloes ten Bhömer, Marios Schwab, Global Color Research Ltd, Mika Nash, Sophie Copage, Winni Lok, Jean-Pierre Braganza, Hannah Maughan, the Royal School of Needlework, Jessica Lecomte, Bernhard Willhelm, Stylesight, Jasper Chadprajong, Julia Krupp, and La Petite S*****.

Thank you to my talented Ravensbourne students for sharing their work in this book: Emma Wright, Clio Peppiatt, Emma de Vries, Charlotte Harris, Leanne Warren, Annie Ovcharenko.

I would especially like to thank Val Furphy for her amazing collection of vintage Comme des Garçons and her lovely prints. Justine Fox for her intuitive colour work in chapter 5. Hywel Davies for his generous and kind support on the first edition of this book, and also those who worked on it at AVA. A huge thank you to Manel Torres, Tina Lutz, Anne Sofie Madsen, James Stone, Duncan Cheetham and Philippa Wagner, for giving up their time to be interviewed.

Thank you to all at Bloomsbury, especially Kate Duffy for her hard work and Helen Stallion for sourcing pictures. Thank you also to the designers ALL CAPS.

Finally much love to my friends and family for their continued support. A huge thank you to my wonderful parents for their endless love and support, and for looking after Wilfred while I worked on this book. To my boys Baz and Wilfred I love you both very much.

The publishers would like to thank Georgina Hooper, Josie Steed and the many designers who contributed images to this book.

Picture credits

p. 3 Patrick Li S/S 2012, photo Christina Smith; pp 7, 9 Catwalking.com; p. 10 jspbdueck/
shutterstock.com; p. 11 © Ashmolean Museum/Mary Evans Picture Library; p. 12 courtesy
Timorous Beasties; p. 13 Mary Evans Picture Library; De Agostini/Getty Images; p. 15 Mary
Evans/TAH Collection; pp 15–19, 21© Victoria and Albert Museum, London/V&A Images; p. 20
courtesy James Stone; p. 22 courtesy Xiao Li RCA graduated collection; p. 24 W10 Handknitted
wool/Alpaca courtesy Nikki Gabriel, photo Anthony Chiappin; p. 25 Kyuchi; p. 27 © Biocouture
2013, photo Bill Waters; courtesy Brooke Roberts, photo Philip Meech; p. 29 courtesy Annie
Ovrachenko; p. 30 © Clio Peppiatt; pp 31–2 Emma Harriet Print Design; p. 33 courtesy A-lab
Milano; p. 34 courtesy Emma de Vries; p. 35 courtesy Duncan Cheetham; p. 36 Catwalking.com;
p. 39 Emma de Vries; p. 40 courtesy Duncan Cheetham; pp 42–3 Emma de Vries; p. 45 Slaven
Vlasic/Getty Images; p. 48 Gamma-Rapho via Getty Images; p. 49 courtesy Christian Wijnants,
photo Bettina Komenda; p. 50 Fernanda Calfat/Getty Images; p. 53 courtesy Rory Crichton; p. 56
AFP/Getty Images; p. 57 courtesy Marloes ten Bhömer; p. 59 courtesy Anne Sofie Madsen; pp
63–4 Catwalking.com; p. 66 courtesy Mika Nash; p. 68 Furphy Simpson; p. 69 Gamma–Rapho via
Getty Images; p. 71 Lou Dalton Menswear; p. 73 FGF industry SpA; p. 75 courtesy Manel Torres/
www.fabricanltd.com, photo Alvaro Diaz; p. 77 courtesy Sophie Copage; p. 79 courtesy Jessica
Leclère/www.jessicaleclere.com, photo Rory Van Millingen; p. 87 Fashion design and
photography: Johan Ku; p. 88 Sonia Rykiel sketch and knit swatches; p. 91 Mathieu Drouet for
Xavier Brisoux; p. 92 mg/Shutterstock.com; p. 93 courtesy Leutton Postle, photo Christopher
Dadey; p. 95 courtesy Nanna van Blaaderen, photo Pablo DelFos, represented by Manja Otten
management; Sapsiwai/Shutterstock.com; p. 96 Dress Eleanor Amoroso, photo Gabriella De
Martino; Laura Theiss, photo Oggy Yordanov; p. 98 Marloes ten Bhömer; p. 99 Manel Torres/
wwwfabricanltd.com, photo Alvaro Diaz; p. 101 courtesy Lutz & Patmos; p. 103 Charlotte Grace
Georgina Harris; p. 105 Gamma Rapho via Getty Images; pp. 106–7 © Xenia Laffely; 109 Emma
Harriet Print Design; p. 111 Sweatshirts Masha Reva X Syndicate, photo Synchrodogs/Idea,
styling Masha Reva; p. 114 pashabo/shutterstock.com; leoks/shutterstock; courtesy Kenzo;
courtesy Furphy Simpson; p. 115 Digitally printed silk and bamboo silk dress by Lilia Yip, model
Haruka Abe, photo Jessica Kneipp; p. 116 courtesy Spijkers en Spijkers, photo Chris Moore;
p. 117 courtesy Furphy Simpson; courtesy Rory Crichton; p. 118 togataki/shutterstock.com;
pashabo/shutterstock.com; Ashley McGinty/shutterstock.com; p. 119 Emma Harriet Print Design;
karakotsya/shutterstock.com; p. 120 courtesy Hannah Maughan; p. 122 courtesy James Stone;
Royal College of Needlework Collection, photo John Chase; Jenny Adin-Christie; p. 124 Jenny
Adin-Christie, photo Yves Salmon; p. 125 courtesy Alison Willoughby; p. 127 Look 12 from the
Erdem Spring Summer 2013 collection; p. 128 courtesy Marios Scwab; p. 128 Design by Elvira't
Hart, photo Satijn Panyigay; p. 130 courtesy James Stone; p. 132 Leanne Warren; p. 135 Jessie
Lecomte designer, photo Jean-François Carly; pp 136–7 Gavin Ambrose; p. 138 © Global Color
Research Ltd; p. 141 Bernhard Willhelm, photo Petrovsky&Ramone/3D animation: Geoffrey
Lillemon; p. 142 Catwalking.com; p. 145 © Global Color Research Ltd; pp 146–7 © Première
Vision SA/François Durand, Stéphane Kossmann; p. 149 Marni/Butsou Lai; p. 151 Trendstop.
com; p. 155 Yuriy Boyko/Shutterstock.com, Amero/Shutterstock.com, Siloto/Shutterstock.com;
p. 157 courtesy Rad Hourani Inc; p. 159 courtesy Jasper Sinchai Chadprajong; p. 161 courtesy
Jan Taminiau, photo Peter Stigter; p. 163 courtesy Xiao Li RCA graduated collection; p. 164
Catwalking.com; p. 165 courtesy Aina Beck, photo Conan Thai; p. 166 courtesy Jack Bebbington;
p. 169 WireImage; p. 171 Catwalking.com; p. 172 courtesy Julia Krupp; courtesy Leanne Warren;
p. 177 Gamma-Rapho via Getty Images; p. 179 Camilla Breurberg, photo Lukas Renlund/model:
Jonas Pedersen Øren; p. 183 Lou Dalton Menswear; p. 185 courtesy Acne; courtesy Camilla
Breuerberg; p. 187 courtesy Anne Sofie Madsen; p. 188 courtesy Annie Ovrachenko; p. 191
courtesy Aina Beck, photo Dominik Tarabanski.

Courtesy Jenny Udale pp 37, 46, 52, 73, 81, 82, 83, 84, 89, 90, 91, 106, 108, 112, 114, 117, 119,
143, 150, 158, 159, 174, 175, 176, 180, 182

Textiles and Fashion